A Gentle Path

Hey Midge—

Please please
indulge & steep
in your richness—
the world needs
you into you . . .

Tina

A Gentle Path

A Guide to Peace, Passion and Power

Tina Thomas

BookPartners
Wilsonville, Oregon

BookPartners, Inc.
P.O. Box 922
Wilsonville, Oregon 97070

Dedication

Sometimes our heroes can be those we teach,
those who take our message and live it fully.

This book is dedicated to my son, Matthew Thomas Bernard, whose life training began in utero when I would take my stethoscope from nursing school and place the ear pads on either side of my belly and whisper into the mouthpiece, "Hello, son, this is your mother." Matthew, whose name means "gift from God," was raised by the principles presented in this book. I cannot begin to describe what a wonderful gift from God he is...truly an inspiring human being.

Thank you, Matt.
With all my love,
Mom

Acknowledgments

I would like to thank the following people for helping me to bring this book to completion. Thanks to: Barrie Mowatt, who was the first person in my life to see the book in me. My "sister," Sheila Grisset-Morgan, for being the midwife to this book. Curt Boudreaux, my book buddy, whose trust in me, and willingness to do what he said he would, encouraged and inspired me. Claudia Gordon, Anne Teachworth, and Rita Breath for living what they taught me. Nanny (a.k.a. Patty Beard), for typing and retyping about thirty this-is-the-last-one versions. Mom and Dad, for being the giants upon whose shoulders this book stands. Marcia K., for asking me the questions that gave this book its shape. Greg Gasperecz, the epitome of balance; all I can say is *Aieeh!* Ursula and Thorn Bacon, for seeing the diamond in the rough and supplying the tools for polishing. Eric Schulze, for standing at the beginning with me. Thanks also to all of my family, friends and clients who have cheered me on and have been so encouraging and supportive.

Table of Contents

Preface

I created this book to save you a lot of time. I have spent my entire life studying people, motivation and communication. This book is a result of over twenty years dedicated to integrating information from many areas of science, psychology and spirituality. What started out as an interest became a passion and then a mysterious key to realms of possibility I had never imagined possible.

I began my work as a life coach by teaching college students how to use visualization techniques to improve their grade point averages. I guaranteed students that if they stayed with my program for six weeks, they would have at least a letter grade improvement or I would refund their money. I never had to return a penny!

One of my students was on the golf team and began to dramatically improve his golf along with his grades. Shortly thereafter, his golf coach stopped by and said, "Hey, I hear you are doing some weird things with my boy; we need to talk." He was initially skeptical of someone who made her living by talking. I was equally uncertain about anyone who thought walking long distances after a tiny ball was a way to have fun. Despite our differing perspectives, the coach and I agreed to work together on his golf game. Much to his surprise and my delight, he became the National Amateur Golf Champion that year and attributed his success to our work. Through this experience, I grew to respect and appreciate the game of golf, which is in many ways like the game of life.

Shortly thereafter, Tulane University Medical Center offered me a position as director of the Cancer Counseling Center and asked that I apply the same principles to people with cancer that I had used with students and athletes. Having never before worked with cancer patients, I considered it quite a challenge and accepted the position. The second patient I worked with was a forty-three-year-old woman who was told by her doctor that she had an inoperable cancer and would live only six to eight months, if she was lucky. We worked together to visualize her recovery and to heal unfinished emotional issues. Three months later, she began to respond to treatment, and eight months later, she was free of disease.

I was in awe of the powerful nature of this work and felt somewhat overwhelmed by the responsibility involved. I became concerned that I didn't know enough about what I was doing. It was like discovering the power of electricity without understanding the physics behind it. To better educate myself, I attended trainings offered by leading experts in the field of body-mind health, such as physicians Bernie Siegel, Carl Simonton and Elisabeth Kübler-Ross. After my training was complete, I realized that no one really knew how this process worked. But it was clear that indeed it was a very powerful process, which often produced far-reaching and unexpected results. Many of these results were nothing less than miraculous. Eventually I realized that this work wasn't about my knowledge or talents, but about coaching people to access their own knowledge and inner resources. Finally, I realized that the same principles can be applied to people who are physically healthy and who want to explore new realms of possibility and discover more peaceful, joyful and elegant ways of making their dreams come true.

If you are open to the possibility of an easier, more elegant, dynamic way of living, with less effort and struggle, this book is most certainly for you. If you are dedicated to your personal growth and committed to improving your relationships, this book will help you to become healthier in all aspects of your life. As you practice the principles in this book you will notice that you feel lighter and more energized, and experience greater satisfaction with life. As you continue to practice, you will notice an enhanced sense of spiritual awareness and the ability to more quickly and easily create the life of your dreams. You may even create a life beyond your wildest imagination!

This book gives you the basics about how your brain works and how to retrain your brain to create more peace, passion and power in your life. However, I do not believe this process works simply by walking through the steps in the right order. I believe that in order for this process to work, you must be open to grace, and enter into this work with a questioning, childlike heart, asking for guidance and trusting that you will be answered.

Webster defines grace as "the love and favor of God toward man." Grace is that little extra energy that wells up so deeply from inside of us that I cannot help but think it is the point where man and angel meet, where physical laws are bent and miracles of love and healing occur. It is that undissectible moment when we have enough information, fear, hurt, pain, courage, trust, hope, despair and inspiration, in whatever combination we need at that moment, to get out of our own way and allow something inside to shift, release and be forever changed.

As change occurs, you will notice that you will be able to go beyond intellectual understanding of the principles in this book, and to embrace them and incorporate them into your life. When you do, you will be awed by the dynamic nature that you and your life will assume. So, as we say down South, "here's the grits," and remember, you'll have to ask for the grace.

Introduction

How to Use This Book

Balance is the key to becoming the most peaceful, passionate and powerful person possible. The balance required for the optimal inner fitness necessary to create peace, passion and power is exactly the same kind of balance required for optimal physical fitness. Optimal physical fitness requires a balance of strength, flexibility and cardiovascular conditioning. You are not physically balanced if you are able to bench press your weight, yet unable to bend over to tie your shoes. Or—what good is having the flexibility of rubber bands if you are out of breath after climbing two flights of stairs? Surely, being able to hike for hours indicates good cardiovascular fitness, but if you lack the strength to carry groceries from the car to the kitchen without straining, your body is out of balance.

One of the challenges to optimal physical fitness is the tendency to gravitate toward those elements of fitness for which you possess some natural ability. For example, I tend to be flexible, so when I took up yoga, which involves a lot of stretching, I was quite pleased with myself. I felt great about my ability to quickly become proficient at flexibility-demanding postures. The down side, of course, was that I avoided strength postures and muscle development, even though I knew they would give me a better all-around body. I simply didn't enjoy being average to below-average in those areas.

Sooner or later, imbalance catches up with all of us. I was no exception to the rule. For more than a decade, I suffered with both a shoulder and a knee that would dislocate suddenly and unexpectedly during sports or sometimes even simple activities of living. The weakness in both joints resulted from accidents that occurred during my younger and more reckless years. I learned to avoid activities that involved risk to those joints and to be gentle with myself during those times when either my shoulder went out of socket or my knee dislocated.

I consulted an orthopedic surgeon, who informed me that although surgery would probably help, it would be costly and require an extensive amount of physical therapy, and the results could not be guaranteed. He told me my joints were "overly flexible" and suggested that strength training might eliminate the need for surgery altogether. My aversion to this type of exercise was so ingrained that I still took a couple of years to get started. I tolerated my situation until one day my shoulder dislocated so severely I saw stars and nearly passed out. That day I made a commitment to begin weight lifting. (It's funny how pain can sometimes be so much more effective than a motivational workshop…) Within weeks, I noticed that my shoulder and knee became more stable and I felt more secure in my movements. My activities became increasingly less limited. Since then, I have rarely suffered with a dislocation of either my shoulder or knee. "Magic!" I thought. "Balance!" I realized. What an empowering moment of awareness for me!

I realized eventually that what holds true for the physical body also holds true for the emotional and spiritual components of our being. As a psychotherapist and life coach, I began to use this knowledge to help people attain greater levels of physical, mental, spiritual and emotional functioning, which are all essential to feeling peaceful, fully alive and powerful. Years of practice in my specialty, psychoneuroimmunology (a formidable title for body and mind health), have led me to understand that no real line can be drawn between the body and the mind. Not only does the mind affect the body and vice versa, but each is an integral part of the other. Neither the body nor the mind can exist or function effectively without the other. Distinctions between the two are arbitrary and used for the sake of convenience. The distinctions I will make in this book are similarly arbitrary. It is important to understand that peace, passion and power are integral, individual parts of each other, and none of them can exist or function effectively without the others. The challenge is to not become so comfortable in one area that you allow the other areas to remain undeveloped. You cannot experience a totally satisfying life without balance.

I recommend first reading the book in the order in which it is presented. After reading the entire book once, I recommend reviewing it in the order in which you are *least* to *most* developed. This will make your progress more balanced and therefore easier.

Please note that all of the people and stories in this book are real. A few examples are composite situations. Names and identifying information have been altered to protect patient confidentiality.

According to the Enneagram*, an ancient guide to personal transformation, moving from an area of strength to a less developed but much needed area for balance is known as moving in the direction of integration. When you are in the middle of your comfort zone it is not always apparent which direction will help you attain balance most gracefully.

*An ancient personality typing system. The Enneagram is a tool for developing compassion and understanding spiritual awareness and growth. It is a system that describes nine basic personality types of human beings. For more specific information read Riso and Hudson's Personality Types or contact the Enneagram Institute at (212) 932-3306, fax (212) 865-0962 or e-mail ennpertype@aol.com.

The following chart is a suggested guide to assist you in determining your order of development:

If current emphasis is on:	Without sufficient:	Symptoms:	Suggested order of development is:
Peace	Power and Passion	Fatigue, boredom, apathy and sluggishness	Power Passion Peace
Passion	Peace and Power	Out of control, chaotic behavior, diffused and scattered thought	Peace Power Passion
Power	Passion and Peace	Lack of personal and relationship satisfaction, restlessness and joy deficiency	Passion Peace Power
All centers	N/A	Present sense of peace, passion and power	Peace Passion Power

In order for you to condition yourself to experience peace, passion and power, you will occasionally see exercises and examples to help you quickly understand and immediately apply this information to your life. Each exercise is designed to give you an experiential understanding of the principles presented. It is the real life application. Once you are comfortable with and proficient in an exercise, you may congratulate yourself for functioning at a higher, healthier level of being. As you condition yourself, you will notice that you are less and less likely to respond to old triggers or sabotage yourself with your former self-limiting patterns.

It is useful and satisfying to create emotional markers or benchmarks to help you track your progress. In a physical fitness program, it is easy enough to see that you are improving your speed or your ability to lift progressively heavier weights. In tracking your personal progress, I suggest that you pay as much attention to the *process* of your growth as the *content*. In other words, the way you respond to yourself when you do or do not take action is just as important as the actual action you take, if not more so. (Of course, everyone goes through slump periods when we do not perform as well as we know we can.) Remind yourself that the ultimate goal of this work is self-acceptance and compassion. To achieve this goal, we create a loving, nurturing and empowering internal environment for ourselves.

Because belief systems, thoughts and emotions are internal processes, it is more difficult to gauge progress in them than in external processes. Many of my clients have found it rewarding to write about their thoughts, feelings and actions during the implementation of the exercises. They are amazed to see the significant changes they accomplish in such a short time. Self-acknowledgment and self-praise are powerful reinforcers and accelerate personal growth exponentially.

One more important note: I cannot overemphasize the importance of consistent practice. Running around the block once or twice does not constitute physical conditioning. Similarly, practicing these principles haphazardly or sporadically will not give you the results you hope to obtain. *Only consistent effort will produce significant results.* While some exercises will be easier than others, concentrate on your undeveloped areas for optimal balance.

As in any fitness program, I caution you to use your judgment. As with all new physical exercises, these internal exercises may cause some discomfort or soreness as new behaviors and attitudes are practiced. If any of the suggestions in this book cause extreme discomfort, please do not push past your limits. I recommend that you practice these exercises in moderation, building in frequency and intensity over time. It is okay to skip an extremely uncomfortable exercise altogether. You may find that doing the other exercises and increasing your tolerance in those areas will enable you to come back to one that initially seemed uncomfortable or unattainable, and to find success.

Joe Weider, known internationally for his work with bodybuilding champions, reminds new athletes that reaching the highest level of bodybuilding involves becoming sensitive to one's body. This basic principle applies to everyone, but each of us has idiosyncrasies. He encourages his bodybuilders to be sensitive to and honor their individuality. This program is no exception. I strongly encourage you to adjust these exercises and principles to meet your own needs for optimum mental, emotional, and spiritual health.

If you get off track, remember that you are developing a mental memory similar to the muscle memory of athletes. Muscle memory refers to the ability a muscle develops to remember the strength, flexibility, balance and coordination required to complete a complex exercise. For example, adults usually remember how to ride a bike even though they may not have ridden for many years. Our muscles remember the coordination needed. A similar phenomenon occurs mentally as well. This is because practicing these exercises creates new neuropathways, or mind maps in your brain. The more often you follow an exercise, the less effort and thought you require to master it. The next thing you know, you will do it automatically. Under stressful conditions you may occasionally stray from practicing these principles. But when you return to them, you will quickly regain your sense of balance and the ability to create your life as you desire.

This book was created as an easy-to-understand guide to creating and balancing peace, passion and power in your life.

Chapter 1, "The Language of Peace, Passion and Power,"

discusses how words and tonality affect physiological and emotional states. Drawing from the field of neurolinguistic programming, you will learn how to understand the languages of peace, passion and power while reading the remaining chapters. This will greatly enhance your ease of mastering these principles and potentiate your efforts.

As you will learn in Chapter 2, "Peace," much of what interferes with our experience of peace in our day-to-day living is a result of the conflict between what we consciously think we want for ourselves and how we unconsciously keep ourselves from getting what we want. You will learn to recognize recurrent themes of failure and frustration and learn how to deprogram the unconscious beliefs that sabotage your happiness. You will also learn how to reprogram your beliefs to support a healthy and successful life. Although the process is deceptively simple, it utilizes some of the most powerful and dynamic tools for change available in the field of human potential development.

Chapter 3, "Passion," describes how to develop a positive emotional attitude in which all emotions can be experienced in a healthy way and describes the dangers from overuse of a positive mental attitude (PMA). You will learn about the positive intention and constructive expression of emotions that will allow you to fully experience passion.

Chapter 4, "The Seven Most Misunderstood Emotions," discusses the traditional definitions of positive and negative emotions as well as a suggestion for new definitions. This new paradigm for understanding emotions sets the stage for experiencing emotions constructively. In this chapter you will learn how to avoid what I call compound emotions, which result from being critical and judgmental of your spontaneous and natural feelings. We will explore the seven most misunderstood emotions (anger, depression, jealousy, fear, sadness, guilt and joy) and discover their positive intentions and how to interpret these emotions in a positive way. As you learn to anticipate these emotions as gifts, with insight you will be able to turn your emotional blocks into building blocks to help your dreams come true.

Chapter 5, "Power," describes power as an internal experience, which, as it develops leads to an increasing ease in influencing your external circumstances.

Chapter 6, "Training the Brain," is designed as a reference chapter for readers who have no experience with meditation techniques. This chapter includes terminology associated with brain training, a test to help you determine your current skill level, basic how-to information, brain training tips and my all-time favorite visualization, which you can modify to meet your needs. For readers who are experienced with meditation techniques this chapter can serve as a quick review or may be skipped entirely.

Chapter 7, "Permission to Be Less Than Perfect," sets forth some suggested guidelines for maintaining a lifelong perspective on living these principles in the real world. This chapter is a reminder to you that all of the information presented in the book is to be taken in the context of your humanity and inherent imperfection. You are encouraged to see yourself not as a self-help project, but rather a work of art in progress. The concepts of embracing imperfection and honoring less-than-productive down time are presented. Also, I ask you to remember that a very important key in creating balance is to allow the process to unfold through awareness and intention rather than by forcing yourself to become balanced.

What's In It for You

This book is your personal genie in a bottle. Whatever you intensely desire, you can create.

Phil, a forty-two-year-old realtor who had never made more than twenty thousand dollars a year, intensely desired to create more wealth but felt like something in his life was preventing him from being as successful as he imagined he could be. He came to see me because just having a positive attitude wasn't working. He knew there must be more to creating the life of his dreams than just thinking about it. As he put it, "I started to feel negative about positive thinking. I began to question myself, like maybe this way of thinking worked for others but not for me." I shared the concepts presented in this book with Phil. Although they were a little difficult for him to accept at first, he began to practice the homework assignments given to him each week. By the end of the year, Phil was thrilled to see his efforts pay off when his income tax return reflected a one-hundred-twenty-thousand-dollar year! The next year he made nearly four hundred thousand dollars. As I am writing this book it looks like he will triple that amount.

These same principles will work for you in the areas of health and sports. Allen, a fifty-four-year-old businessman, was diagnosed with prostate cancer. He used the principles in this book to better deal with having cancer and coping with treatment. Not only did he not suffer the side effects of treatment, but, after complete recovery, he decided to use the same strategies to improve his tennis game. He went from never qualifying for a local tennis tournament to winning the tournament two years in a row.

Finding love and creating healthy relationships is also possible. Sue Ellen, a thirty-six-year-old secretary, was afraid that her biological clocking was ticking faster than her ability to find someone she could love and trust. She had a horrible history of broken dreams and broken hearts. She probably never would have attempted this work had it not been for the success of one of her dear friends, Bob, who was a client of mine. Bob convinced her that if I could help him attract the love of his life, I could easily help her. Although skeptical, she was willing to give it a try. Nine months later she found love with an incredible man. Two years later she married Mr. Incredible and became the mother of twins. (I'll bet there are days when she tells others to be careful about what they ask for!)

Peace, passion and power in your life are rewards enough in themselves, but in the process of creating them you become much better at living the life of your dreams. You have the ability to become your own genie.

Unlike the classic genie in a bottle, you are not limited to merely three wishes. However, you do have one condition: You must understand that you are the only one you can change and your life is the only life you can change. This book is not about how to change or fix others.

Once you decide to put your efforts into helping yourself, and to follow the guidelines set forth in this book, you will find that this particular path is simple and gentle, and produces dynamic results.

There are basically seven stages on this path. The stages do not always occur in neat order. Sometimes you'll skip a stage or two. Sometimes there is overlap. Sometimes you may be working on all stages simultaneously at different degrees of intensity. The stages are as follows:

1. Freedom from negative unconscious belief systems. Your experience of the world is shaped by your beliefs. Much of what you believe is related to deep-seated and unconscious imprints that can sabotage even your best efforts at success. This book will teach you how to reprogram these imprints. By removing negative, unproductive imprints, you can come to love your original self— which is essential for complete healing. The original self is the pure essence of your unique being-ness; it is who you were and what you were meant to be before you were taught who you aren't. As you discover and accept your original self, you will be able to observe your imprints more objectively. When you can see your imprints as something you learned, and not a part of your original self, you will be positioned to more easily and gracefully rework these imprints. Acceptance of your original self without upset is the foundation for peace. Reworking imprints reinforces that peace.

2. Decreased internal stress. As your imprints are reworked into healthier more authentic images of your self and the world, you will find yourself feeling less self-critical and less judgmental of others. An internal ease will emerge, and you will notice that life becomes less of a struggle. Although your circumstances may fluctuate in the natural rhythm of life, with its cyclic ups and downs, you will experience a greater sense of internal peace. You will probably notice that your life begins to take on a gentle, flowing quality in ever-increasing ways.

3. *The transformation of emotional blocks into building blocks for building your dreams.* Your heart contains the dreams that express your true and original self. As you learn how to read your emotions you will begin to understand that although you *experience* your emotions, *you are not your emotions.* Emotions have a language of their own; they are messages from your heart that let you know whether you are living authentically and in alignment with your original self. The keys to unlocking your dreams are hidden behind the unpleasantness of many threatening emotions. Even unpleasant emotions such as anger, guilt and jealousy carry important positive messages. By extracting the positive intentions of the seven most misunderstood and distorted emotions you will lessen the fear associated with dealing with them. As you understand how they serve as important messengers pointing the way to your dreams, you may actually look forward to experiencing these emotions.

4. *More frequent experiences of joy.* As you learn to embrace threatening emotions, their negative charges diminish. You will experience fewer of them, allowing more time and energy for joy and contentment. Before you know it, you will move beyond merely accepting your original self to actively expressing your original nature throughout all aspects of your life. As a result of expressing your true self, you experience more joy and more passion.

5. *Unconditional love of self and others.* As you understand your emotions more clearly, you will understand other people better. Greater depth of understanding will lead to an ever-increasing sense of compassion for yourself and for others. Your love will become unconditional, meaning that you can love yourself or others as-is and without certain conditions. This creates a more honest and safer space for relationships and better communication.

Not only does this lead to intimacy and connection with others, it also creates the opportunity for a sense of intimacy and connection with life and all that is. Many consider this state of love and connection the entry level to spiritual awareness.

6. *Fine tuning of your ability to turn dreams into reality.* Exercising personal power is actually the easiest part of this journey. Once the foundation for peace and passion has been established, you will learn the simple formula for balancing action with intuition. This will allow you to live in a spiritually creative partnership with the universe. Or call it God, Mother Nature, Higher Self, or whatever term you feel most comfortable with. With the grace from this partnership, your dreams will more easily become reality.

7. *Greater ease in creating and maintaining a balanced and satisfying life.* You will then discover how to access your centers of peace, passion and power for a more elegant means of decision making. This will greatly reduce the tension and angst that hinder you from creating the life of your dreams.

I hope that you will embrace all of the above with a gentle and loving attitude. Embrace your humanness and imperfection as you practice these principles, because *how* you proceed on your journey of self-discovery and growth is as important as the journey itself.

As you practice this gentle path of compassion, you will be awed by the grace and dynamic nature that you and your life assume. Use this book as a guide to empower yourself on your journey of life.

I offer my services as a life coach to you today, just as I do to clients in my private practice. For us to work together, I recommend the following agreement. I have, to the best of my ability, presented this information in simple terms, and I have been as honest and authentic as possible. For your part, please agree to suspend any doubt that you have concerning the principles presented or your ability to implement them effectively. I ask you to trust in my experience and know that as surely as your body responds to any regular, physical exercise program, your mind, spirit and body will respond to this mental exercise. If you practice these principles every day for the next three weeks, you will notice a significant difference in your energy level and your outlook on life. In three months or less, you will see significant differences in your life circumstances and in your ability to influence them. Remember that although you don't have to believe in water to get wet, you do have to jump in.

You may be asking yourself how I can be so confident about this. All I can say to you is that I no longer merely believe these principles work. I know they do. I know it because I live this way in every area of my life and I have been a witness to the powerful, transforming, life-enhancing nature of this work in the lives of many others. And I will enjoy hearing from you one day, when you tell me how you applied these principles to dramatically improve the quality of your life. My hope is that you will catch the contagious, enthusiastic spirit with which this book was written and that the rest of your days will be filled with more peace, passion and power than you can possibly imagine.

1

The Language of Peace, Passion and Power

The words we use in our everyday language have the power to shape our experience. I first learned this years ago, in nursing school, when one of my instructors overheard my fellow nursing students and me discussing how much we dreaded working with Mr. Smith, the most difficult patient on the ward. "There's no such thing as a difficult patient," she told us, "only a patient with difficult problems." She then encouraged us to find the source of Mr. Smith's difficulty. We agreed to, and discovered Mr. Smith's biggest difficulty was his having seen in his chart a doctor's notation that read "S.O.B." Mr. Smith did not realize that S.O.B. is medical shorthand for "shortness of breath" and not a derogatory remark. Once we discovered this misunderstanding, we all had a good laugh along with Mr. Smith.

We learned an important lesson that day. From then on we approached all of our patients with a very different attitude. No longer did we feel threatened by "difficult" behavior. We searched until we found the source of difficulty. Sometimes it was pain, at other times it was fear or stress. When we approached the patients in a nurturing, encouraging and nonjudgmental way, they were receptive and we always discovered a reason for their seemingly incomprehensible behavior. Our entire experience of people changed dramatically by changing the label "difficult patient" to "person with difficult problems."

I learned from that experience to choose my words more carefully. I now enjoy rainy weather a lot more because I describe it as cozy rather than dreary. I feel less stressed when faced with a challenge rather than a problem. And I actually enjoy red lights and stop signs because I now call them reminders to breathe and relax.

Not only does a change in a word affect your emotional state, we are now learning that your choice of words also affects your body. Every single word you use produces a physiological response in the body. Every single word! Can you imagine that? In the past few years, my work with biofeedback equipment has contributed immensely to my understanding of how important it is to pay attention to what we say to ourselves. Biofeedback equipment measures muscle tension, heart rate, blood pressure, respiration, and even the electrical charges that occur on the skin from moment to moment.

After the system is set up, I ask a series of questions to enable my clients to see on the computer screen how their bodies respond to their own words and thoughts. This system creates the opportunity to experiment with alternate words and thought patterns that will decrease stress levels in the body. Some words and thoughts are very powerful and produce big waves on the computer screen. I'm sure it will come as no surprise to you that words associated with love, sex and money are among the most highly charged. (You can bet advertisers have known this for a long time!)

Do you know one of the toughest words to use on your body? Do you have any idea? Well, you SHOULD! The imperious, imperative word "should" creates a contracting, restrictive effect on your body, mind and spirit. You don't have to take my word for it. Your body is constantly giving you bio- (or body) feedback. To experience this, close your eyes for a second and think of some task you do not particularly enjoy. As you close your eyes, tell yourself how you really *should* do that unpleasant task real soon. Notice what happens to your body. Most people notice a flat, pressured or deflated quality. Not something you look forward to, is it? Now, close your eyes and tell yourself you *could* do that unpleasant task real soon. Notice what happens to your body. Most people sense a light, expansive, almost playful quality when using the word could. The task may become a little less unpleasant as well.

You can do the same thing with a pleasant experience. Think of an experience you enjoy, then close your eyes and tell yourself how you really *should* do that again soon. Notice what happens to your body. I think you get the idea. Even in regard to something pleasant, you may find yourself resisting "should" with as much passion as a dog will resist something forced down its throat. It doesn't matter if you are forcing medicine or its favorite doggie treat, it is the force the dog resists. It is the same kind of reaction we may have when an authority figure tells us in an overbearing way what to do. Our response is "Oh, yeah, you think I'm gonna do something I don't want to do. Not on your life, buddy! Nobody tells me what to do!" Similarly, if we get too pushy with ourselves or try to force something on ourselves (even though it may be good for us or what we truly want), our internal dialog will sound like "Oh yeah, you think I'm gonna do something I want to do? Not on your life, buddy! Nobody tells me what to do, not even me!" We end up not doing the very thing we want. We'll show us, won't we!

I know many athletes and people in all walks of life who reach an invisible ceiling or barrier to success. Try as they might to drive through these invisible barriers, not until they take a gentle, more compassionate route are they able to allow themselves to be drawn to their goals and rise above the limitations they struggled against for so long. Take the group of world class runners who, during their practice runs, were asked to run at nine-tenths of their usual effort. They did so, and in the process set new personal best times. The runners were incredulous! They could not believe they had beaten their best times with less effort.

Certain that a timing error had occurred, the runners asked to repeat the trials. Sure enough. Less effort, better results. They discovered that by not pushing so hard and relaxing into the run, their muscles relaxed, giving them longer and more efficient strides, which improved their times. If you are not achieving a goal in work, relationships or health, you may find yourself saying, "I could do this if only I tried harder, or had more discipline, or was stronger." Perhaps the key is to spend some time eliminating harsh and overbearing words and to replace them with words and phrases that nurture, excite and empower you.

Not only what we say to ourselves, but how we speak to ourselves is very important. I discovered that even when we say the right words, if we use the wrong tonality we end up sabotaging ourselves without even realizing how! Peace, passion and power each have a unique language consisting of distinct words and tonality. As your awareness of your self-talk increases, you will notice that certain words and tonality become amplified. You might even find it a little distracting at first. A former client insisted that every time she heard herself say "I *should* do this or that," the *should* sounded twice as loud as the rest. This is a good sign and not something to get worried about. After all, you can't slay a dragon if you can't see it.

Also, remember to be kind to yourself as you go through this process. Another client of mine said that when she decided to give up her negative self-talk, she didn't speak to herself for a week because she didn't know what to say. The more fluent you become in each area, the more easily you will be able to access these states consciously. Eventually, you will find that you automatically relate to yourself in words and tones that support greater and ever-growing amounts of peace, passion and power.

How to Speak Peace

The opposite of forcing or attacking is nurturing. Watch a loving mother encourage her child to take a first step. She'll say, "Come on son, you can do it." Her voice is soft and gentle; her tone is soothing and comforting; her words are positive, encouraging and supportive. "It's okay, I'm right here. Come on...I know you can. Just let go of my hand....There you go. Mommy's right here. That's my boy, good..." The child goes for it. "Good..." He does it! "Oh yes!" She claps her hands in delight. "Good for you! I'm *so* proud of you."

Imagine the same situation with a mother who has poor self-esteem and does not know how to love and nurture herself, much less her child. This mother might say, "All right, you little rug rat. Let's see what you can do." Her voice is harsh and perhaps on the loud side. Her tone is irritating, grating, and somewhat pressured. Her words are negative, discouraging and destructive. "Go on, do it. What are you afraid of? Think you are going to fall on your little can? Go on, do it. What's the matter with you? Are you chicken? Hurry up, let's get this over with so I can take this picture." He is going for it. "Come on, hurry up." He falls. "Damn, a ruined picture. At this rate you are *never* going to walk."

While it is hard to imagine that someone would talk this way to another, it happens all the time. And many times we unconsciously speak to ourselves the same way. Unfortunately, the part of our brain that evolved earliest (the limbic system) can become paralyzed with fear and unable to accomplish what it wishes to accomplish.

Take the case of Bob, a tennis pro who had reached an invisible ceiling of performance. When he came to see me for help, he told me that he already had worked with a psychiatrist and had taken care of his emotional and mental blocks, yet his performance limitations remained. He had experienced no improvement. In fact, his game had worsened. From experience, I've learned that when you make a positive internal shift, positive external results appear. Always—with no exceptions. I asked him to describe the nature of the particular problem affecting his game. "I told you," he snapped. "We already figured that out. The problem was that I beat myself up every time I made a mistake." I suspected from his answer that he was still trying too hard and was still being tougher on himself than he realized.

Because there was no apparent change in the tennis pro, I

suspected that he was unaware of how roughly he was still speaking to himself. "Can you just tell me what runs through your mind when you make a mistake?" I asked him. He became even more agitated with me and repeated, "I told you, I already took care of that problem! Every time I make a mistake and start to beat myself up, I tell myself, 'Stop it, stupid! You're beating yourself up!' But my game hasn't improved at all." Because he had had no nurturing role models in childhood, he was not conditioned to self-nurture. This young man truly believed that he was doing the right thing in the right way.

At first, I thought he must have been joking, but his expression was so pained and confused, I soon realized that he was not aware of the brutality of his attempt to be kinder to himself. I see this situation often in people who tend to be drivers for perfection. They push themselves mercilessly, and when they fall short of their ideal expectations, they assume the problem is that they are not self-disciplined enough and need to push harder.

However, the opposite strategy is the antidote to this situation. The solution is a gentler, more patient, nurturing approach. An increase in self-nurturing as opposed to self-pushing or self-discipline is the healing balm needed to counter this problem. As you add more nurturing to your internal dialog there is less room for the fear and tension associated with pushing yourself unfairly. As fear and tension diminish, goals can be accomplished much more comfortably. When someone has a problem caused by lack of nurturing, that person will experience a shift in circumstances when he begins to nurture himself. Sometimes it is a dramatic shift.

I suggested to Bob that he listen to my tone and my words as I spoke to him in a loving, compassionate and nurturing way. He tried to model my example, but had difficulty adjusting his tone at first. From his harsh and aggressive stance, this nurturing tone sounded "wimpy" and he was concerned that it wouldn't be "stern enough to get top-notch results." But because his way had proven ineffective, he agreed to be kinder to himself. Instead of cursing himself when he lost a point, he would say to himself, "That's okay. That was a tough shot. I'll get it next time." Within weeks, his tennis game improved significantly and so did his life!

As amazing as it may seem, you too can improve the quality of your life when you learn how to be gentle with yourself, especially when you make mistakes. Practice developing a tone that says, "Aw, that's okay…You'll get there, I know it. Yes, that is it! Good for you! Way to go…I am so proud of you." Speak much the same way as you would to a two- or three-year-old entrusted to your care. It may seem silly at first, but it is very powerful reconditioning.

If you are not sure of how well you nurture yourself, especially when you make a mistake, try this exercise (it might surprise you): Listen to yourself when you drive in traffic! No kidding. The degree to which you can be gently nurturing and understanding with others when they make a mistake is the degree to which you can be kind to yourself when you are under fire. When we are critical of others, it is as if we have given them a photocopy of our self-criticism and kept the original, which is always just a little sharper and tougher than what we send to others.

One last comment on self-deprecating comments. Sometimes when I point out the negative and self-effacing things people say to themselves, they respond by saying, "Oh, I didn't really mean it that way," or "I was just kidding." The catch here is that the earliest-evolved part of your brain doesn't always understand kidding and too often takes the message literally. So please speak kindly to yourself. You'll do that for yourself, won't you?

Negative Words and Phrases to Avoid
- I am so stupid.
- What a dummy I am! I can't believe I did that!
- What's wrong with me?
- I am a jerk! Look what I didn't accomplish.
- Yes, but I made a mistake.
- That's just my kind of luck.
- Yes, but it is not perfect.

What are your most commonly used negative words and phrases?

Positive Words and Phrases to Add to Your Vocabulary
- I am proud of me.
- Good job.
- I am doing fine.
- That's okay, I'll do better next time.
- Well, look at what I've learned.
- I'm good enough.

What positive words and phrases would help you?

Nurturing Language

Listen to the negative words that critical and unhappy people use. Count the number of negative and positive words and phrases you hear in a minute. Repeat the same listening exercise with gentle and loving people. Are you surprised?

Work on eliminating your negative, self-defeating, self-effacing words and harsh, critical and abrasive tone in traffic jams, where it is easy to hear your words and tonality. This will automatically transfer to the other areas of your life.

For the icing on the cake, consciously compliment yourself with positive nurturing words and phrases at least once an hour.

Because negative self-talk is an unconscious habit, I recommend a buddy for this exercise. A lot of my clients tell me they *should* stop saying "should." And I have had clients who were convinced they were free of negative words and then repeated the very words they were working to eliminate twelve to fifteen times an hour without even noticing.

How to Speak Passion

When it comes to destroying an openness for passion, I know of no better way than the "been there, done that" syndrome. When we determine beforehand that any person, experience or day is going to be dull, predictable or boring, and then choose words to match our attitude, we are setting ourselves up for that very experience. It reminds me of the time I worked in the medicine clinic of a huge hospital. My job was to take the blood pressure of everyone who came to the clinic and give a specimen cup for a urine sample to each diabetic patient. My office was tiny and had no windows. I found myself referring to it as the "dungeon" and calling the clinic a "meat market" and my position the "most boring job in the world." I often found myself grumbling, "Another day, another dollar." After two months of this attitude, even weekends lost their pleasure because they meant Monday was right around the corner.

Finally, I decided to make an attitude adjustment. I decided that the challenge of this job was to find the challenge, and sure enough I did. I began to think of my office as a little "storefront for love." I would then try to see if in my limited time with each patient (approximately two minutes), I could inspire them or make a difference in some small way. One day, for example, I was able to coax a smile out of eighty tired and stressed-out patients. What an accomplishment! Furthermore, I noticed that my little "storefront" started to feel larger in size and brighter, though to my knowledge no one had changed the light bulbs. I realized that if I could find passion in the "dungeon," anyone could find passion in their lives anywhere. When you realize this is true for you, you can eliminate all those words and phrases that brainwash you into believing that today is just another day. Same-old, same-old. Been there, done that. (Yawn.) Need I go on?

In addition to the "been there, done that" syndrome, passion-sapping words to avoid include implied demands and commands. I once worked with a runner who was having difficulty motivating himself. While connected to my biofeedback equipment, he described his morning this way: "Well, I wake up and say to myself, 'I really have to go run.'" The screen revealed a flat line. No energy. Nothing happening. I asked him to change that "have to" to "get to." The words "have to" have an oppressive quality; the words "get to" have an almost privileged connotation and create a sense of anticipation or enthusiasm. He tried it: "I *get* to run."

As he said the words the biofeedback screen began to reflect a bit of excitement. When he saw that, he continued, "Yeah, that's it, I *get* to run! Some people have to work nine-to-five jobs. Some people can't physically run at all. But not me, I get to run whenever I want to. I'm a pretty lucky guy!" His eyes lit up along with the indicators on the screen. Bingo! He realized that the missing ingredient for his workout was gratitude. He had taken his program for granted until it had become routine and boring. By changing his words, he was able to instill new life into his running program.

Not only do the words we use affect our ability to create passionate states, but so do the tones. In fact, tonality directly affects our level of passion and enthusiasm. Talk about excitement! Positive tonality becomes the exclamation point to your words. It energizes you and your words at the same time. Most people notice a lift or surge of energy. It's a boost you can give yourself throughout the day. It can make the difference between feeling passionately alive and merely existing.

Take the case of Tony, a sixty-eight-year-old man who had prostate cancer and was very depressed. He had been depressed for about three weeks when he came to see me. "What's the first thing you say to yourself when you wake up in the morning ?" I asked him. "Well, let me see. I never really gave it much thought. I guess the first thing I say when I wake up is, 'Well damn, I'm a cancer patient.'" I told Tony that if I spoke to myself with the heavy, draining tone he used, I would be depressed too, no matter what words I chose. "Let's play around with your tonality, or *how* you speak to yourself. How about keeping the words, but changing the tone?" I suggested. "Let's see what happens." When we met again the following week, he looked ten years younger! I asked him what had happened. He smiled sheepishly. "I took your advice and I changed my tone! Now every morning when I wake up I say, 'Well damn! I'm a cancer patient!' Next thing you know I'm thinking, 'I better get what I can get out of life while I still can!' Then I find myself popping out of bed like a piece of toast from the toaster!" Seven years later, he is still doing fine. Pay attention to your words *and* your tone. It can make all the difference in the world!

Enhancing Passion

To enhance passion:

Read the following phrase out loud in a flat, monotone voice: "Good job. I'm proud of you." Now imagine that someone you respect is telling you this in the same flat, monotone manner. Feel the response in your body. (If you pay attention as you do this exercise, you will be able to notice a response.) Now read the same phrase out loud in a very enthusiastic tone: "GOOD JOB! I am proud of you!" Imagine that someone you respect is telling you this in the same enthusiastic way and feel the response in your body. Notice any difference?

On low energy days, notice how your words reflect your attitude and how your attitude is affected by your words and tonality. Eliminate from your repertoire all the draining "been there, done that (sigh...yawn)" words and tonality. Add passionate words and phrases to your vocabulary when describing your internal states (for example, "I'm excited, enthused or jazzed") and when describing other people and situations: "She's incredible, amazing, powerful and dynamic!" "That's super!" "It was fabulous!" Although it may feel awkward at first and somewhat forced, within weeks your actions will match your words. Before long your feelings of passion will follow your actions. Practice spicing your language with enthusiastic words and energetic tones in front of a mirror. Notice how you look more attractive physically. I know this sounds silly, but it works.

See whether you can become enthusiastic in situations that are normally associated with boredom or frustration by talking to yourself in an encouraging and enthusiastic way. Remember, sometimes the challenge is to find or create the challenge.

All the passionate words in the world won't make a bit of difference if you are not cultivating your passion and honoring your feelings. Words and tonality cannot substitute for honest enthusiasm, but they can amplify your passion when you are purposeful.

How to Speak Power

Truly powerful people don't need to prove it. The words and accompanying tone that they use reflect a calm and confident presence. I learned this lesson years ago while walking on a beach with a friend of mine named Robert, a big, gentle, teddy bear kind of a guy. I told how vulnerable I was feeling because several of my girlfriends had been victims of violent crime in unrelated events. My sense of security was shattered. As a woman (and five foot four), I saw myself as small and powerless. "Why, if I had your body," I said, "I wouldn't be afraid of anybody! I would just walk anywhere I wanted to and beat people up and nobody would mess with me!" Robert replied, "Maybe that is why God made you little."

As I reflected upon his words, I began to notice that truly powerful people do not walk around attempting to intimidate other people by loudly announcing how powerful they are. I have never heard the President of the United States boast, "With my little finger, I could start a nuclear war." I don't need to prove to you that gravity exists, it does. When I am truly confident in my abilities, I just am. My great grandfather always said "If you want to know if a man is a man, give him a little power." How many times that has proven true. Real power, very much like truth, does not have to prove itself.

While the tone of peace is soft and sweet and gentle, and the tone of passion is exciting and enthusiastic, the tone of power lies somewhere in between. Power words are words of action and phrases of commitment, such as "I will make it happen," "I'll take care of that," "Consider it done," "I'll handle it," "You don't have to worry about that, the buck stops here," and "I'll do it." Neither overly sweet nor overly enthusiastic, power tones are quiet and resolute.

My client Jerry, a rather boisterous and verbose man, revealed in one of our sessions that he felt like a phony. He was always trying to impress others with what he knew, how much money he made and how much power he had. But in the end, he felt less powerful. Jerry spent most of his time entertaining people and doing what others expected him to do. Exhausted, miserable and feeling like a failure, he came to see me because he was "tired of being the jester." I recommended that if he didn't want to be a jester, he could practice being the king. I asked him to imagine himself as someone with true power, like a king in his own kingdom. Jerry agreed to give it a try and began to eat as he imagined a king would eat, to speak as he imagined a king would speak, and eventually to think as he imagined a king would think. He became much less pressured to prove his power. Instead of talking about his power, he lived it. Although he remained friendly, he seemed quieter, more thoughtful and less anxious to please others. "A true king," he said, "is gentle and wise and has nothing to prove." His speech became less pressured and his laughter less forced, and the words he used were fewer in number but closer to the point. I believe it was no coincidence that his peers and family members began to treat him with much more respect. As a bonus, he noticed that customers who had been put off by his old style were approaching him for new business. I occasionally see Jerry and when I ask how he is, he smiles shyly and says, "It's great to be the king!"

Self-Empowerment

To enhance self-empowerment:
1. Observe the negating words that unempowered people use. Words that sap power include *try*, *can't*, *never* and *but*. Phrases that keep us victimized include "I have always been that way," "It's my nature," and "I can't change." Count the number of negating versus empowering comments you make in a day.
2. Eliminate negating and disempowering words in your vocabulary.
3. Add positive, empowering words and phrases to your repertoire. Power words include: *challenged* (as opposed to *overwhelmed*); *opportunity* (as opposed to *problem*); *possible* (as opposed to *impossible*); *can*, *will* and *must* (as

opposed to *can't*, *try* and *might*). Power phrases include "I can," "I will," "Consider it done," "No problem," "Failure is not an option," and "Just do it."

Note: Because negative, disempowering speech is an unconscious habit, I recommend asking a buddy to help with this exercise. Ask a trusted friend or loved one to gently point out when you use negating speech.

4. If you find yourself bragging or boasting, ask yourself privately why you are feeling unsure or insecure. Be kind to yourself and you'll get where you want to go sooner rather than later.

2
Peace

Peace: the ability to be clear, content and free of judgment in the midst of a situation or emotion.

Learning Who You Are Not

Have you ever wondered why, as an intelligent human being, you do things that don't make logical sense, even though you know better? Most people who smoke, overeat, under-exercise, or have chemical or relationship addictions detrimental to their health know better. Even though they are smart enough to know these behaviors are self-destructive and may consciously attempt to stop these habits, they don't.

Take, for example, Mary. She is a twenty-eight-year-old single woman who desperately wants to be in a committed relationship. She hopes to have a couple of children before her midthirties. Mary is grossly overweight and reports that unless she loses a significant amount of weight, she feels too unattractive and uncomfortable to date. She feels miserable about her condition. She knows what she needs to do to feel good about herself but after work she skips the gym workout she promised herself she would do (for the hundredth time) because she feels embarrassed and self-conscious about her size. She feels so bad about herself and not keeping her commitment, by the time she gets home, that she heads straight for the DoubleStuf Oreos to comfort herself. She feels horrible but she is unable to call someone to talk about it. She's waiting to make friends until she can get a grip on her life. As Mary goes to bed she tells herself tomorrow will be different. Tomorrow she will start her exercise program. She hopes so, anyway, but she has a sinking feeling that tomorrow will not be any different.

Have you ever wondered why some business deals fall apart, not for logical business reasons but because someone was threatened by the way the deal was handled and decided to "take his marbles and go home" for no apparent reason? Take the case of Joe, a struggling businessman who canceled his involvement with a major firm because he didn't like the way he was treated at the company Christmas party. Joe thought that because he was doing a good job, he should be treated with special respect. He resented the company president's critical attitude. According to Joe, the president was just like Joe's father, always seeing what was wrong rather than what was right. Joe's bowing out was a major loss for Joe and the firm. Funny thing though, everyone else at the party thought the president was very complimentary, especially of Joe! Later, his wife would comment that every time Joe discussed the Christmas party incident he would assume the whining tone and posture of a five-year-old child. Is it possible that Joe saw this experience through the eyes of a hurt child? He wonders how his career would now be different if he had seen the event in the same way as his peers.

Have you ever seen a promising relationship ruined when one or both partners regressed into childish behavior? How can a mature successful adult slip into name calling or temper tantrums when he doesn't get his way? I once counseled a couple in their midfifties, each with a Ph.D., who were considering divorce now that the children were grown. The source of their conflict? They were embarrassed to admit that most of their disagreements were over Fluffy, their aging cocker spaniel. *He* thought Fluffy needed more freedom. *She* thought Fluffy needed more attention. Seems silly, doesn't it? Or does it?

If you try to understand these scenarios from a logical perspective, you will find yourself frustrated and confused. The reason you cannot figure yourself out logically is because humans are not logical creatures. You are capable of logical thought, but what drives you is an emotional and irrational part of your unconscious brain, which operates with a logic of its own. Once you crack the code to this part of your brain you will find that emotional and motivational issues that have stumped you for years can easily be understood and reworked to your advantage. But what is the code? How do you make sense out of irrational behaviors and beliefs?

How do you stop a battle between two forces you can't see? On one hand, you consciously want what's best for yourself and those you love. On the other hand, an unconscious force seems to take over and cause you to say, think, or do things that undermine your success. This internal battle between your conscious and unconscious mind disrupts your sense of peace and is exhausting. Not only does it wear you down, but you end up using all of your energy just trying to stay sane. If you were no longer in conflict with yourself (the conscious self versus the unconscious self), not only would you consistently experience more peace, but you would also be able to use your energy to move forward and accomplish your life's dreams.

A first step toward reconciling these two selves is to understand that you basically operate with two brains at the same time. I am sure you have heard a lot about right brain and left brain thinking. The left brain refers to the left hemisphere of the brain that is logical and better with numbers and spatial orientation. The right brain is more creative and better with words and language. There is another, more powerful way, however, of mapping the brain in terms of function. It also divides the brain into two separate regions. The two halves are the front brain and back brain. You might also call them your conscious brain and your unconscious brain. The point is that they have two separate ways of processing information, and optimum mental health is related to how well these two brains communicate and work with each other. Once you understand that your brain has two minds of its own, it becomes your job to utilize each to its maximum potential in a harmonious way.

The front brain is the cerebral cortex, the huge area of gray matter located in the front and midportion of the skull, also known as the new brain or the human brain. It encompasses both left and right sides of the brain, which means it is rational and imaginative. It perceives time as past, present and future. This brain thinks in terms of words and numbers. The front brain is the conscious part of your brain, the part that you are aware of when you think. The front brain's ability to be self-aware separates us from all other creatures and is considered a distinctly human feature.

One way of gaining control of some of your uncomfortable emotions is to understand that you have the ability to choose how you think, and to realize that how you think can influence your emotional response. These conscious thought patterns originate in the cerebral cortex, the thinking part of the brain. If you think that someone is attacking your character when he or she gives you feedback, you will respond by feeling hurt or angry. If, however, you choose to interpret the feedback as a loving gesture, and acknowledge the time and effort taken to share it with you, you will more likely feel loved and appreciated. By changing your thinking pattern, you experience a more comfortable, healthier way of feeling.

When you see an error in your perception of a situation or individual, you can alter your perception and no longer be bothered by unpleasant feelings in that area. Changing your thought patterns can quickly and easily become a conscious process once you focus attention on it, which is how you change front brain patterns. Such cognitive understanding is not sufficient for dealing with all emotional states, however, because not all feelings are generated by thoughts. The feelings that are generated immediately and without conscious thinking follow the back brain pathway. These feelings are primitive and happen quickly when protective action is needed and there is little or no time for thinking. An example of such a feeling is a startled response to seeing a spider on your shoulder.

The back brain, a little V-shaped section called the limbic system, lies on top of the brain stem at the back of the skull. Its primary function is to keep the body alive. Because its function is so basic and primal it is also known as the old brain, the reptile brain, and the survival brain. The limbic system is considered the emotional brain because all strong emotions originate in this area. If, for example, a brain surgeon were to probe in this region, you might laugh hysterically, sob uncontrollably, or express deep rage. This system is basically unconscious, which means that you are not usually aware it is operating. However, when you focus your attention on it, you can often become conscious of its function and what messages it is giving or receiving. The limbic system does not think in terms of time. There is no past, present, or future; it thinks only in the present, here and now. This here-and-now awareness coupled with strong emotion is the basis for survival. When you were a hungry baby, you didn't think, "Oh, Mom fed me about two hours ago, so she ought to be back in fifteen minutes. I can wait." Instead, you felt hungry and got very emotional. Your emotional cry gave someone the message, "Hurry up! I'm hungry. I've got to eat or I will die!" You screamed. Eventually someone heard your frantic plea for survival and gave you a breast or bottle. Then you were okay, at least for a while.

As an adult, it doesn't work that way anymore. Often, patterns that worked well for us when we were children handicap us as adults. When we get overly emotional as adults, for example, others might say, "Hey! Back off! Get a grip. Deal with your own stuff!" and move away from us rather than give us what we are screaming for. Most adults don't realize that if they are upset and fearsome on the outside, it actually means the emotional limbic system is feeling hurt or scared. Worse yet, if you haven't learned about the way the back brain thinks and communicates, you will be inclined to use your front brain to criticize your behavior that doesn't make sense to you. This process creates bad feelings and begins a vicious cycle that shreds your self-esteem. After all, if you don't like yourself and can't motivate yourself to change, who will? What you need is improved communication between your front and back brains.

If you can imagine a parent in the driver's seat and a child in the backseat, you can begin to appreciate how your brain communicates. The cerebral part of the brain is like a parent. It is very adult and is supposedly in charge at the wheel, with a particular destination in mind. The back brain, on the other hand, can be as distracting as an unruly child in the backseat. Consider a child who doesn't want to go to the doctor's office and creates such a ruckus that the adult is forced to pull off the road for fear of creating an unsafe situation. The back brain has similar power. Our tendency is to ignore the childlike back brain, especially when we have a particular goal or destination in mind and want to get there in a logical and adult fashion. However, sometimes what we consciously think we want (front brain goals) and what we unconsciously create (back brain desires) are very different, resulting in self-sabotage, failure and pain.

It has become popular in recent times to refer to the back brain as the "inner child," because of its childlike nature. Don't be fooled by the term "child." Despite its childlike responses this part of your brain is an integral part of your physiology and happens to be the oldest and the wisest part of you. It knows who you were before you were taught who you are not. It is always the most powerful determinant of whether or not you will move forward to fulfill your dreams. Whether you like it or not, a six-year-old kid is really the chairperson of your emotional board. It may seem unfortunate to have a six-year-old kid in charge of your emotions, but if you recognize the truth, it can be used to your advantage. If you ignore the truth, ridicule it, make fun of it, or even deny its existence, you may find that you will be forever taking the scenic route to reach your destinations in life. The scenic route is not necessarily a bad route, but it is indirect. I want you to know you have another option, a more direct, joyful, elegant and compassionate and less stressful route. This route is known as the back brain pathway.

The back brain pathway is one of the most powerful, dynamic, and awesome opportunities for change that I have experienced. It is deceptively simple, as well. It is based on reprogramming imprints in the limbic system, through the process of imagination, to produce immediate change in the way we feel and behave. What is an imprint? Imprinting is a process that occurs in individuals of every species during the impressionable time in early life when they are conditioned or programmed with a world map. Once developed, your imprint determines who you are, who you aren't, and what your world is all about. For example, when a duckling emerges from its eggshell, the first moving thing that it sees becomes "Mom," regardless of whether it is a duck or a dog. If its real mother isn't around at hatching time that little duckling may spend the rest of its life trying to be the best Labrador retriever it can be.

Obviously, the imprinting process creates a very strong template from which we see the world and ourselves for the rest of our lives. In a revealing study, a litter of kittens was raised in an environment where all they saw were horizontal stripes for the first three weeks after their eyes opened (corresponding to their imprint time). When these kittens were introduced to the real world, they ran into table and chair legs because, as far as they were concerned, vertical elements didn't exist. I often wonder how many possibilities and opportunities we do not see because we know "I'm not that kind of person," or "I don't like those kind of people," or "That kind of luck happens to others, not me."

Paulette and George

Paulette, a miniature poodle, was the alpha (most aggressive and dominant) puppy in her birth litter. When it was time to eat, Paulette ate first, and when it was time to sleep, she chose the most comfortable spot.

George, a German shepherd, was the omega, or runt puppy, in his birth litter. When it was time to eat, George ate last and when it was time to sleep, he ended up with the spot no other puppy wanted.

Both Paulette and George were to be weaned just before Christmas, and as fate would have it, each was selected as a Christmas surprise for the Anderson family. And what a surprise it was! Mr. Anderson had taken great care to see that his wife and children had no idea that he was bringing home a miniature poodle, his wife's favorite kind of dog. Mrs. Anderson had noticed that her husband seemed disinterested in her hints to get a poodle. She decided, in the spirit of Christmas, to surprise her family with a German shepherd pup. After all, Mr. Anderson had talked for years about getting a shepherd.

On Christmas morning, the children were awakened by not one, but two yelping puppies, and were delighted to find Paulette and George under the family Christmas tree. George was already three times bigger than Paulette, but the children quickly noticed that Paulette was the first to eat Christmas breakfast. During the day, George made a few feeble attempts to assert his dominance but was quickly put in his place by Paulette. By Christmas night, Paulette slept in the choice sleeping spot and George took whatever was left.

As a full-grown dog, George was twenty times the size of Paulette, but he would cower whenever she growled at him. At any moment, of course, he could have stepped on her and shown her who was boss. But in his mind, Paulette was the boss, always had been and always would be. Paulette lived and died as an alpha dog and was buried next to George, the eternal runt.

Unlike cats and dogs, which have a relatively short period of time in which imprinting occurs, the imprint period for humans continues for five to seven years. This is enough time to get a lot of inconsistent, distorted, and unhealthy messages. The good news is that you get to keep your positive imprints forever. If your parents gave you messages like "We are glad you are here," "You will always be loved," "There is no such thing as failure, only feedback," and "You are capable," you will keep those messages, have a high sense of self-esteem and live in a world that reflects that you are a wonderful person. You will attract people who hold you in high regard. You will treat the world in an open and loving manner. And the world will respond to you in kind, at least most of the time.

The bad news is that any negative imprints you have will be unconsciously played out again and again. Ask any adult over thirty years old and most will admit that life has become a series of events in which the names change but the themes stay the same. Imprinting not only conditions a person to perceive who they are, it also creates their perception of the world and life experiences. If a girl grows up in a home which the father abandons (either physically or emotionally), she may well grow up believing she can't trust men. This girl will become the kind of woman who goes to a party and always is attracted to a major loser, an untrustworthy man. If she accidentally joins with a trustworthy man, she will project mistrust, saying things like "You said you were getting home at ten. It's now ten-thirty. Where were you? You don't really expect me to believe that story, do you?" Eventually, she will drive this man either away or crazy. He will either abandon her or live down to her expectations (and at least get credit for what he is being blamed for.) Her response? "See, I knew he couldn't be trusted."

All of us have imprints that result in patterns of behavior that are self-destructive or limit growth and fulfillment in some way. These imprints arise from hurtful previous experiences or childlike misinterpretations of reality, which then become part of an internal map of our world. This map contains the code or blueprint that tells us who we are, what we are capable of, what our limits are, and how we expect the world to treat us. This is not a logical map, but an emotional map, which creates its own illogical rules.

From these rules evolve certain themes. I refer to these themes as unfinished business, because until they are resolved they will be repeated in our lives, over and over again. If you've been around the block of life a few times, you will notice that although the names and exact circumstances may change, the themes themselves are familiar.

Can our themes be altered in such a way as to assist us in creating a healthier, happier and more peaceful life? Absolutely! But how? The key lies in understanding that the brain doesn't make a distinction between what's real and what's vividly imagined, and the limbic system doesn't make a distinction between past, present, and future. Therefore, if in your imagination you can go back in time and create an alternate past, you can also create an alternate present with an alternate future.

Healing negative imprints is greatly aided by therapeutic visualization. I have worked with clients who, after spending years in analysis and psychotherapy with little progress, healed from a variety of past emotional traumas in a matter of a few weeks through visualization and the reprogramming of their limbic imprints. When distressed by an unproductive theme in your life you can go back in your imagination to your childhood and change your history by giving yourself new information. This process is similar to changing tapes in a stereo system. If a stereo system is playing scratchy tapes, you don't throw out the stereo, you replace the tapes with newer and better-sounding ones. In the same way, more often than not, there is nothing wrong with us except for some screwy imprints (beliefs about ourselves, money, relationships, etc.). It is far better to give ourselves new, improved messages to live on than to dismiss ourselves as wrong or bad or unworthy.

Angela, a forty-three-year-old woman whom I counseled years ago, was distressed because she was unhappy with her life. Always dressed in muted and drab-colored clothing, Angela spoke softly in barely a whisper. "I feel horrible all the time," she said. "My life isn't what I want it to be, but then I can't really put my finger on what I really do want." I made a couple of attempts to explore imprinted messages but was unsuccessful since Angela was unable to recall any childhood memories. After a few sessions during which she expressed her concerns, she began having repeated spontaneous images of cake doughnuts. The images would appear in dreams, while she was driving, or during work. Although she was haunted by the images, she didn't understand what they meant and why they appeared. To explore the situation, I guided her into a relaxed state and a related childhood memory appeared. In this memory she was five years old. She described the scene like this: "I am five years old and I am stupidly telling my father that I don't like cake doughnuts." Her comment struck me as odd. What is stupid about saying that you don't like cake doughnuts?

She assumed it was stupid because her father responded by

grabbing her by the throat, pushing her against a wall and screaming, "You don't like cake doughnuts? This is all we have to eat and you better like it or else!" Given the consequence, I understood how a five-year-old child would consider what she said to be stupid.

I asked Angela to imagine her adult self, dressed as she was, entering into the scene and giving her child self and her father new information. She replayed the scene again, with the child telling him she didn't like cake doughnuts. Just as he went to grab the little girl, her adult self stopped him and said, "What she is doing is a good thing. She is just saying what she wants. Maybe you are doing the best you can, but hurting her is not acceptable. This child needs love and respect." She then took the little girl by the hand, walked out, and said, "From now on I will take care of you." And she did.

When Angela went home that evening, she was met by the familiar sound of the television. She had been married for seven years and her husband habitually kept the television on, even when he was not watching it. She realized she had never liked having the TV on when she arrived, but she had never told her husband. Her fear was that he would respond negatively and she would get hurt. This day she walked in and told him she did not like to be greeted by the TV. To her delight, he agreed to make sure it was not on when she arrived. Her reprogramming had produced a tangible positive result for her within twelve hours! When he asked her why she had never mentioned it before, her truthful response was, "It never occurred to me that I had the right to say it."

She then began to assert herself in a more positive way in all aspects of her life and liked the way others responded to her. She was especially pleased with her husband, who began treating her more romantically. He even began to brag to his friends about what a "spunky" woman Angela was becoming. Once Angela became comfortable asking loved ones to help her, she began to realize she had a right to ask for what she wanted from life. She and her husband built their dream house in the country and adopted two precious children. She learned how to do pottery, started her own home business—and learned how to belly dance. The last time I saw her I hardly recognized her. She was in super physical shape, wearing a glamorous outfit in eye-catching bold blue. Her voice was clear and strong. She radiated joy.

Angela's experience demonstrates how this type of imprint alternative is a very dynamic and powerful process indeed. It is a Gestalt-like approach that takes advantage of the limbic system characteristic of not distinguishing between past, present, and future. The limbic past is changed by adding a healthier alternative, resulting in greater chances for changed behavior in the present, usually within twelve to seventy-two hours. This approach deals with the "fire" of an issue, rather than the psychoanalytical "smoke."

Because emotional healing through the limbic system is so powerful, it is helpful to understand some of the characteristics of this type of work. One of the most important is the distinction between an associated state of recall and a dissociated state of recall. In the associated state, the past event is experienced in a firsthand manner; the events and experiences are viewed and felt from the perspective of the inner child. In the dissociated state, the events are observed from outside the inner child, as if the adult self were watching the scene. Most people find that recalling traumatic experiences in a dissociated state is emotionally easier than rehashing the trauma in an associated state in which they experience the event as if it is happening to them again. On the other hand, if you are seeking to enhance a positive experience from your past, it may be more powerful to do so in an associated state, making the adjustments you feel are helpful.

An important characteristic of inner child/limbic work is that it creates an alternative to the original imprint, but it does not erase the original imprint. In order to sustain the positive results, you then consciously access the alternative imprint by recognizing the positive behavioral shift, sensing the positive feeling associated with it and looking for other opportunities to apply and reinforce it. If you do this frequently enough, the alternative imprint becomes the natural feeling-to-thought pathway that guides your perception and beliefs, thus creating the more desirable outcomes chosen.

Remember that the child's attention span is short and it must be gently reminded of the available alternative until the new choice becomes the natural pathway.

The childlike self must choose to embrace the alternative imprint. We cannot consciously force its choice. Fortunately, the original self inherently understands loving, healthy intentions. It will almost always choose a more loving, safe, and secure way for itself. This usually takes practice on the part of both the conscious and the original selves to build internal trust. If a person was emotionally harmed or abused as a child, the adult self treats the original self the same way he was treated by caretakers. The healing occurs as the adult and the original self move together to a more loving, compassionate and trusting relationship. This is reflected in the adult's behaviors, choices, and treatment of self. As the trust relationship builds, the adult makes safer, happier, more joyful and more satisfying choices for life.

Another characteristic of inner child work is that it can be used to access the inner wisdom that our thinking (front brain) selves have clouded. This was illustrated for me when I was in graduate school. I was doing poorly in statistics and feared failing the upcoming final exam. I was frantically cramming for the test when I spontaneously imagined my little-girl self standing next to me, tugging on my skirt, saying, "I want to go swing." Well, at that point I panicked and thought, "Oh my God, I have lost it. I am now hallucinating my inner child at inappropriate moments! It's time for me to turn in my mental health card." But I was so stressed and so curious about this spontaneous phenomenon that I decided to go to the porch and see what this was about. As I was on the porch swinging, I began to relax and noticed that my shoulders were coming down from my ears. I felt more comfortable and I remember saying to myself, "Hey, you know, I don't know what I'm so worked up about anyway. If I fail this final, it is just another semester of school. No big deal." Then in my imagination my little-child self was sitting next to me again and said, "Another semester of school? Yuck! Let's go study."

Now what is really almost embarrassing about this story is

that when I went back to the statistics book, I noticed that the information stuck to my brain like a magnet. It was so easy to understand that it began to seem like remedial statistics. Before relaxing, I had been so anxious that I failed to see the ease of the course. The wise child-self knew that I needed to relax, and in a childlike way, it unconsciously communicated to me to swing myself back to a relaxed state of mind.

My swing experience is an example of how the child-self can guide the adult self to a greater sense of fulfillment. But the reverse situation is also possible. That is, there are many instances in which the adult self is the only one who can guide the child-self to safety or new possibilities. Such was the case when, as director of a cancer counseling center at a hospital, I arranged to receive some specialized training. I was excited about the opportunity and mentioned it to some of the oncology nurses. Later, I overheard them talking about me. They were saying how wonderful I was and how exciting it was that I would be able to get the training I wanted. I was very proud of myself and just ready to enter into the nurses' station to enjoy their praise when one of the nurses said, "Well, who does she think she is? She's just a nurse like the rest of us." I had an immediate heart and gut reaction. I felt very embarrassed and small. I wanted to shrink and disappear. I literally had my back to the wall as I slid down the hallway back to my office. I didn't return to the nurses' station at all that day.

That evening I felt very uncomfortable before going to sleep and asked my unconscious to help me find out how I had learned this feeling. It seemed to be way out of proportion to what happened at the nurses' station. When situations that don't seem to warrant a strong emotional reaction occur, it's a good indication that some issue in the unconscious limbic system has been triggered. So I asked my unconscious to go back in time to find my child-self—to a time or incident that may have been the cause of my strong emotional response. Normally, I would go back to where I grew up as a child. The scenes would usually be events that happened in my home or my neighborhood. But in this particular instance I found myself in my second grade classroom. At first I thought my unconscious mind made a mistake. Why would I imagine myself in second grade? I thought that perhaps I should start over, but decided to trust my back brain and follow my imagination to a scene that I had long forgotten.

I was walking back from the teacher's desk after just being told I would be the leading female character, Mary, in the school Christmas play for the third year in a row. I was so proud that I thought I would burst. But while walking back to my desk, I heard my little girlfriend say, "Who does she think she is? She's just a second-grader like the rest of us." It triggered the same feeling I had at the nurse's station. I wanted to shrink and disappear into my desk. I felt so awkward and embarrassed. So, in my imagination I took my adult self back to the child-self and told her, "What these little girls are feeling is jealousy. Jealousy can be a good feeling because it means they see something in you that they want to become." She was very relieved and said, "You mean I don't have to feel bad for feeling good?" I promised her that she didn't, gave her a big hug, and told her that I was proud of her. The next morning I went to the nurse's station and saw the nurse who seemed to begrudge me. I felt fine and was able to gently suggest that her reaction could be an opportunity for growth. It turned out to be so, but that's another story.

When doing limbic system work, look for the elements and symbols of what your child is telling you, not necessarily the literal meaning. For instance, if your child-self says to jump off a bridge, you wouldn't take it literally. As a metaphor, it probably means it is time to make a change or jump into a new opportunity. I learned this the very first time that I did inner child work. I made contact with little Tina Marie, who asked me to listen to her needs. She asked me not to ignore her or put her off. I promised her that I would listen whenever she made contact with me. Later, I checked in and asked her how she was doing. She said in her cute, little-girl way, "I want to go to Florida." Then I panicked because I had just promised her that I would do what she wanted. But it was a Sunday and I had school on Monday so it wasn't possible for me to go to Florida.

So I began to think of the elements of Florida: water, wind, and sun. I told my husband, "Come on, we're going to Florida." I took a sheet out in the backyard, put on a fan, and played some ocean wave tapes. We laid out in the sun, drank lemonade, and for all practical emotional purposes, were in Florida. When I checked in with her, she was enjoying "Florida" and was very happy that I had kept my word.

Of course, you may sometimes find it necessary to explain that you cannot do what your inner child wants exactly when he or she wants it. Other things can, and sometimes should, take priority. Just be honest about the situation and keep your promises to yourself. If you commit to something to be done later, it most likely will be fine. But make sure you follow through. If you do, you will gain the trust of possibly your most important ally in life—YOU! When you know that you will be there for you no matter what, whether you win or lose, through sickness and in health, in good times and bad, for richer or poorer, you will have a true appreciation of unconditional love and peace.

Practice Makes Possible

1. Identify a recurrent theme that sabotages you.* It can be related to recurring statements you make, such as "I knew this would happen" or "Why am I always the one who...?" Themes can often be uncovered when your reactions are out of proportion to the situation: "This is my kind of luck," or "I'm never the one who..."

   Note: Sometimes this one is difficult, because we are talking about an unconscious process. There may be times when we are so entrenched in an issue that it takes an objective observer on the outside to help us see our unconscious blind spots. Dream work can help if you enjoy it and intuitively understand how to listen to your unconscious messages. But if you are caught up in the middle of an issue and can't find relief in one to two weeks, consider looking for a Gestalt therapist or a credible hypnotherapist. We can all benefit from an extra bit of coaching now and then.

2. Trace the theme back to the first memory, experience or impression. You can experiment with the Healing Your Child-Self Visualization and adapt it to meet your specific needs. If, for whatever reason, you cannot recall an actual event, you can make one up. Sometimes the actual memory or experience is extremely traumatic or you may simply be trying too hard. Relax and trust your imagination. The unconscious has an amazing capacity to create an episode for healing that will be perfect for you.

3. Bring your adult self into the scene. I usually recommend bringing yourself dressed as you are in the present moment.

4. Give the child-self new information. It is usually information related to a distorted perception. If you don't know what to say, ask the child what he or she needs to hear. Healthy self-esteem and child-rearing books can give you some ideas of positive messages. So can a good therapist.

5. Continue until you experience a physiological reaction. Reactions can include but are not limited to: crying, being able to breathe more easily, flushing, feeling relaxed or relieved, sighing, having a sense of feeling lighter, and laughing.

6. Look for external shifts. You may notice changes: in the way you describe the past event or similar present and future events; in the way you react to a similar situation; in the way people respond to you; in your awareness surrounding similar events.

7. Reinforce your new programming by congratulating yourself, and find opportunities to apply the alternative imprint. *This is not only extremely important, it is the most often overlooked step.* Remember that this step is what helps you to keep the benefits of your effort for the long term.

Healing Your Child-Self Visualization

To do this visualization exercise more easily, you might want to record the following script on a tape recorder and play it for yourself at a time when you will have no interruptions. The slash marks (/) are a reminder to pause briefly.

Allow yourself to relax in a comfortable position. / You may want to uncross your arms or legs. / If you'd like to, you may close your eyes. / Let go of any tension you may be aware of in your body or mind. / Slow your breathing down. / Allow your breath to deepen. / Take a deep breath and hold it. / Feel the tension it creates across your chest and body, / exhale, and gently say the word "relax" to yourself. / Allow each inhalation to bring you energy and peace, and with each exhalation release any tension or negativity that you may have accumulated during the day. / Releasing, / let go, / allow your muscles to unwind and relax. / If you notice any noise in your environment let it merely remind you to let go and relax more deeply. / Now imagine a wave of warm, soothing, healing energy moving down from the top of your head, to your face, around your eyes, to your mouth, releasing your jaw, and relaxing your tongue. / Feel this wave of warm, soothing, healing energy moving down from the back of your neck, throat, and shoulders, moving into your chest, upper back, middle back, lower back. / Feel this wave relaxing your heart, lungs, stomach, abdomen, buttocks, thighs, knees; warm, soothing healing energy relaxing your calves, ankles, feet, and toes. / (Sigh.) Take another deep breath and hold it. / Become aware of the tension you create by holding and release, exhaling gently and saying the word "relax" to yourself, as you are already in an even deeper state of relaxation of body and mind. / Imagine yourself now entering an elevator, not an ordinary elevator, but a very special one designed just for you. / In this elevator is a cushioned recliner, which is molded to fit every inch of you perfectly. / Relaxing into the recliner, you feel it support you gently and firmly, like a loving cloud. / As the elevator door closes, relax and see the number ten above the door. / As you watch the number ten change to nine, feel yourself letting go, relaxing more and more deeply, completely. Feel any residual tension that you have, releasing and letting go. / As you see the number change from nine to eight, sense the peace and calm within you. / You are quiet and serene. / See the number eight changing to seven. Lucky seven, / lucky you. Remind yourself of the many blessings you have. Feel yourself breathing those blessings in. See yourself surrounded by the abundance that you already have. / See the number seven changing to six. / See the number six changing to five. Five sounds like alive. Remember times when you felt most alive. Breathe in that energy and aliveness. Feel that total sense of well-being. / See five becoming a four. / Four changing to three. / Three sounds like free. See yourself as free to be who you really are. Becoming more and more every day that which your spirit calls you to be. Free to make your dreams come true. / See the number three changing to two / and two to one. / As you arrive at the first floor, the doors open up onto your own personal and private beach. / Totally secluded and safe, as you walk out, you feel the sand beneath your feet. You see the ocean waves and hear the gentle song of the ocean as the waves rock you rhythmically to the sound of your breath, / in and out, / in and out. / You see the sky, / the clouds, / the sun; / you may even hear the birds in the distance. / Feel yourself walking with the sun on your back warming your muscles, relaxing you deeply. / Find a spot that is safe and secluded, and as you lay down by yourself to rest more deeply, imagine yourself as a pat of butter on the sand. / Allow the warmth of the sun to massage your muscles and feel any last bit of tension that you may have melting away. / From this relaxed state you gently rise up and in the distance you see a small child. / As this child gets closer and closer you recognize it to be your own childlike self. / As this child approaches pay attention to how you feel toward this child and how this child feels toward you. / Get down on this child's level and ask what it is that you may do to help. / Perhaps you can help by offering a hug, or just being there as a witness. / Sometimes you may need to share new information. / Sometimes you may need to return to past hurts and confusing times to give this child the support and understanding that, for whatever reason, was not available at that time. / You are always free to return to this childlike part of you to check in, tune up, and heal. / Make an agreement you can keep as to when you will return / and as you say goodbye for now, pay attention once more to your body and what you are aware of inside. / Allow your attention to return to your breathing and to your body. / When you are ready become aware of your back and gently stretch your arms and legs, open your eyes / and return your awareness to your surroundings, feeling awake, refreshed, alive, healed and ready for living.

3

Passion

Expressing Who You Are

Living passionately involves experiencing all emotions to
their height and depth. When I share this information,
many people stop and say, "Well, I don't mind feeling the emotions
I *like* more intensely, but I'm not thrilled about feeling
uncomfortable emotions intensely." Join the club. No one is thrilled
about feeling uncomfortable emotions more intensely. But as far as
passion is concerned it's part of the deal.

Being intimate with your self, others, and life means being
more exposed, more open and vulnerable. When you dance closely
with someone, you're likely to get your toes stepped on from time
to time. When you dance intimately and fully with life, your
emotional toes risk getting stepped on from time to time as well.
The degree to which you feel passion in your life will be in direct
proportion to the degree to which you are willing to experience
some discomfort. Please note that I did not say you will always
have to feel discomfort, but you must be *willing* to feel
disappointment, frustration, anxiety, fear and any other emotion
that may come as part of a full experience of life.

Passion may at times involve a sense of living on the edge,
which requires a willingness to live between feelings of excitement
and fear, much like when you ride a roller coaster. On a roller
coaster, you first experience anticipation—you don't know what to

expect. As the ride speeds up, so does your excitement, gathering momentum, becoming more and more exciting, until it feels like it might go out of control. That's when excitement turns to fear. (Fritz Perls, the founder of Gestalt therapy, believed that fear is speeded-up excitement without sufficient oxygen.) If unchecked, fear can turn to panic, and panic can become paralyzing terror. But as soon as it's obvious that you are not going to derail and die, the fear slips back into excitement. You then get off of the ride saying "Wow! What a ride! How exhilarating. I'll have to do that again sometime!" A roller coaster is a mechanical way to give your body the rush of adrenaline that accompanies feelings of excitement, and a hint of passion as you step off ready to take the next challenge.

You don't have to buy a roller coaster for your backyard, or wait for the next fair to come to town. Any time you willingly and openly step into life you can have a similar experience.

Experiencing and expressing your original child-self is at the very core of passion. The word association that most people make with *passion* is sex. The words that come to my mind when I think of passion are *deep*, *intense*, *powerful*, *profound*, *free*, *exciting*, *wild* and *primal*. Hmm, no wonder so many people associate the word *passion* with sex! But passion related to sex is only one aspect of the much larger and more powerful world of passion, which can permeate all aspects of your life when you learn to listen to your heart. The heart is the place where dreams are born. It helps you stay on purpose in an alive and vital way.

This energy and ability in its raw and energizing form is still evident in children, who are very passionate by nature. Unbridled by social norms, children haven't completely learned restraint. Temper tantrums are passionate and so are play, fear, make believe, and disappointment. Likewise, your passion evolves by allowing your child-self, which has a childlike free spirit, to be fully expressed.

Because you are unique, expressing your child-self may move you out of the neatly packaged label of *normal* or *acceptable*. By definition, being unique means being different. Being different implies change. Change is generally perceived by most people in our society as a threat that brings discomfort. The process of shedding your conditioned self-image and embracing your child-self can involve a degree of discomfort, but the payoff is having an authentic self, a feeling of aliveness, and a renewed sense of excitement in every area of your life! It takes courage to tuck your fear under your arm and be who you are genuinely, whether others approve of you or not. You must take your eggs of self-esteem out of someone else's basket. Sometimes even your own judgment of who you are—and who you are conditioned to believe you *should* be—needs to be reckoned with as well.

When your passion is the result of experiencing and expressing your childlike self, passion becomes much more than just a thrill for the sake of thrills. It becomes a rich, exhilarating, meaningful and joyful experience. Not all passion is experienced as titillating. Intensity is a more accurate indication of passion than is a high or a happy feeling associated with living. Deep passion can actually be a profoundly calming and soothing experience when you are fully immersed in the flow of expressing your heart's desires.

But how do you know what it is that your heart desires? You begin by listening to your emotions. Unfortunately, in our modern world, we have lost touch with the emotional component of our being, the part of us that helps connect us to a sense of our self and our life's purpose. In twentieth-century culture, we value logic and science. Emotions tend to be seen as a hindrance, an aggravation, a necessary evil, or something we ought to rise above.

Many people suffer terribly in their personal and professional lives because they lack an understanding of the positive intentions of emotions, the positive expression of emotions, and the ways emotions become distorted and misunderstood. Many relationships and business deals have collapsed due to misunderstanding of this vital language. Emotions, however, are as necessary for survival as hunger. I know a lot of people who say they wish they didn't have to deal with hunger. They wish they were free of hunger so that they could avoid the health problems associated with being overweight or on a poor diet. But hunger is not the problem. The way we feed ourselves is the problem. Likewise, when it comes to emotions, having feelings is not the problem. Most of our difficulties come from not knowing how to deal with feelings constructively.

We have created negative associations with certain emotions because of the unhealthy ways we perceive and handle those emotions. We blame the emotions themselves for our problems rather than the way we have learned to express them. In a revealing study, rats were placed in very crowded living quarters, where researchers observed that the normally socialized rats quickly became crazy and violent, chewing off each other's ears and tails. The explanation behind the behavioral change is that animals need a certain amount of space and freedom. The unnaturally crowded environment was oppressive and created a stress response that caused the animals to act in unhealthy and antisocial ways. In the same way, when you emotionally oppress yourself, you create an intense stress response and suffer all sorts of dis-ease.

Emotion is the language of the original self; therefore, heed this warning: Too much positive thinking can be dangerous to your health. I know this sounds contrary to popular opinion, but I have seen many people suffer by insisting that their only problem is that they just don't think positively enough. In proper perspective, a positive mental attitude is great for your mental health, but over-emphasis on the power of the mind and the importance of positive thinking risks creating a state of imbalance. Eating broccoli is good for your physical health, but eating broccoli all day long to the exclusion of other foods is obviously not healthy and would lead to a state of physical and chemical imbalance. Likewise, suppressing or denying all feelings that are judged to be negative creates an imbalance that prevents communication with the original self at the cost of emotional, physical and spiritual health.

Overdeveloped PMA

One of the most dangerous ways to emotionally suppress yourself is through overuse of a positive mental attitude. Although the benefits of having a positive mental attitude (PMA) are undisputed, people who have developed *only* the PMA aspects of their personality are unidimensional characters who lack the depth and strength necessary to cope when life isn't just peachy.

Three major problems result from an overdeveloped PMA:

- When you block or deny access to unpleasant emotions, you also block pleasant emotions. All feelings then become muted and nothing is very satisfying. The result is a detached, spectator-like experience rather than an active participation in the experience of life. Blocking emotions reduces intimacy to a concept rather than a shared reality, because emotional expression is the bonding glue that creates a heart-to-heart connection
- Research indicates that unexpressed emotions, pleasant or unpleasant, may actually suppress the immune system, making one more susceptible to all sorts of illness
- Perhaps the most important point: If you fail to listen to the messages from your feelings, you will be unable to hear the subtle voice of your heart. This subtle voice is the key to all of your passion. It is the voice that whispers your dreams to you. Your heart also stirs up unpleasant emotions and creates restlessness to let you know when you are "off purpose" or the emotional needs required for you to live "on purpose" are not being met.

Developing a Positive Emotional Attitude

I believe there is a richer and even more empowered way of living. To begin a journey filled with passion requires mastering a positive *emotional* attitude (PEA). A person with a PEA has learned the value of emotions and has a rich and free-flowing relationship with his or her internal emotional life.

These are the three steps required to create a positive emotional attitude:

- Learn how to access your emotions
- Give yourself permission to express your emotions, which

are indicators of your original self
- Learn how to *interpret* your emotional signals in order to discern whether you are truly living according to your purpose.

Accessing Emotions

Emotions are physical responses felt as feedback to perceptions. Most of these feelings are quite fleeting and subtle. The average person has forty thousand to fifty thousand thoughts a day resulting in forty thousand to fifty thousand chemical reactions and physical responses (feelings) associated with those thoughts, most of which escape conscious attention. These subtle emotions remind me of the clock in my office that ticks softly all day long. Most of the time, its gentle ticking goes unnoticed because my attention is focused on my work. However, now and then, when a client and I are in the middle of a quiet moment, I become aware of the sound of my clock. In much the same way, emotions are changing and shifting and giving us messages about how we feel about what we are thinking and doing. In the noise of everyday life we may not be aware of these steadily ticking responses, but in a quiet moment of awareness we can learn to check in with ourselves and determine whether we are on track with our goals, values and needs.

Taking a few moments out of each day to access emotions can become an easy habit. Not only does increased awareness enrich our emotional experience, but the feedback can be invaluable as well. Many of my clients report that accessing their feelings has saved them time, money, energy and even relationships.

For example, Philip, a thirty-eight-year-old man, told me that once he became aware of his emotions, he was able to avoid a destructive relationship pattern. While dating a woman in whom he was very interested, he noticed a vague sense of hurt and frustration because she never invited him over for dinner (which he interpreted as an intimate gesture). Normally he would have overlooked his discomfort, but he was certain his discontent would have grown and grown until one day he would have blown up over some inconsequential incident and blamed it all on her. By accessing his discomfort he was able to explore his past for similar times when he had experienced the same type of feelings.

He discovered that he had an imprint that was unconsciously working against his well-being. The imprinted message he had learned said, "If I have to ask for what I want it's no longer as good as if it were given to me." He used a combination of front-brain reframing and back-brain reprogramming and was able to discuss his needs with his girlfriend, who had no idea that he wanted to be invited over for dinner. As it turned out, she was happy to comply, although a little nervous about her cooking skills, which was the reason she had avoided asking him over in the first place.

"I can't tell you how many relationships have ended with my being disappointed and angry with a girlfriend but never really knowing why," he later told me. "I was always sure it was her fault and had a list a mile long of all the reasons why she didn't work out. But it was difficult for me to believe after two failed marriages and two failed engagements that I didn't have something to do with this. Learning to access my feelings helped me to uncover my inaccurate and erroneous perceptions of myself, others and the way relationships should be. Not only that, but my current girlfriend and I have the best relationship I have ever had in my life. She says she feels so lucky to be involved with such a sensitive man. When I recall that I almost ended the relationship because she didn't ask me over for dinner, I shudder."

A requirement for experiencing intimacy with others is the ability to access feelings and express them in a way others can understand. Once we become more intimate with ourselves we can more easily be intimate with others. Emotional expression is the glue that unites people intimately. It may take a little while to access feelings if avoiding feelings has become a comfortable habit.

Remember, accessing emotions begins with awareness of their existence. Certainly you've noticed that whenever you buy or consider buying a certain type of car, it seems as though suddenly the highway is full of that particular model! Those cars didn't just happen to arrive when you became interested. It is much more likely that they were there for some time and, as your attention heightened, so did your awareness. The same pattern can happen internally as well. Awareness does not produce emotions, but it does allow you to increase your sensitivity to them. As you increase your sensitivity, you also increase your emotional intensity. As you become attuned to your various emotional states, you may be surprised at how wide a range of emotions you experience on a daily basis. Because of this heightened sense of intensity, pleasant emotions will feel even more wonderful.

It is only fair to warn you that, as your awareness increases, your sensitivity to unpleasant emotions also increases. The good news is that as you learn how to access unpleasant emotions, your ability to release them will also increase and you will be finished with them sooner. I am sure you would agree that it's very difficult to slay a dragon you can't see. Likewise, hiding unpleasant emotions in our caves of denial and repression denies us the opportunity to access them and do something with them. Instead of allowing you to experience an emotion acutely and then let it go, an inability to access keeps you in a chronic state of uncomfortable feelings. Stated simply, the way to get *over* feelings is to go *through* them. If you try to deny or hide feelings, you bury them alive. Eventually, they will leak out to harm your health or relationships.

Separating Thoughts and Feelings

Many people are confused when trying to distinguish thoughts from feelings. When I listen to weather or news reports, I often hear comments such as "I *feel* the weather will be good," or "I *feel* that the Giants will win the game." Actually, these people are stating thoughts. "I *think* the Giants will win the game" or "I *think* the weather will be good" are more accurate statements. As a rule, if you are able to substitute the word *think* for *feel*, you more than likely are expressing a thought. If, however, you can substitute the word *am* for *feel*, you can be fairly certain that you are expressing a feeling. Consider this statement: "I *feel* happy." When I substitute the word *am* (I *am* happy), the statement still makes grammatical sense and I have expressed a legitimate feeling. However, if I say "I *feel* that is a good idea" and substitute the word *am* (I *am* that is a good idea), the statement makes no sense. "I *feel* that it is a good idea" is a sentence that expresses a thought, not a feeling.

To begin to distinguish your feelings from your thoughts and to increase awareness of your emotional states, monitor your speech for use of the word *feel* when you mean *think*, and consciously correct yourself.

To increase your awareness even more, spend ten minutes a day writing down your feelings in a journal or sharing them with someone. To become truly proficient at accessing your emotional states, end your ten minutes of sharing with a five-minute description of how you felt about what you wrote or shared. Underline or highlight the feeling words when you review. Couples may want to correspond with one another.

Consider the following sample journal entries from John and Mary:

> *Dear Mary,*
> *How do I feel about our relationship? Right now I am feeling very <u>frustrated</u>. It seems that no matter what we talk about, it ends up with one or both of us feeling <u>angry</u>. We have been <u>upset</u> with each other for weeks now. I feel <u>nervous</u> now when we have to discuss something. I also feel <u>hurt</u> when I try to express my needs and you act as if you don't think what I'm saying is important.*
>
> *How do I feel about my sharing? I feel <u>sad</u> and <u>lonely</u> when I read my answer. I really want us to be okay again. Remember how we use to laugh at so many silly things?*

> *Dear John,*
> *When I began to read your letter, I immediately felt <u>angry</u> and <u>defensive</u>. "Oh no! Here we go again," I thought. Then I realized that I was feeling <u>hurt</u> too. I didn't know*

how concerned you were about our relationship. I shared your feeling of <u>sadness</u>. Then I found myself feeling a little <u>hopeful</u>. Maybe we do have a chance.

Possible Feeling-Oriented Questions:
- How do I feel about watching a sunset?
- How do I feel about my childhood?
- How do I feel about my mother?
- How do I feel about my father?
- What is the greatest loss I have experienced?
- What is the greatest success I have experienced?
- When did I feel most loved?
- What kind of person am I?
- How do I think others see me?
- What parts of my body do I like or dislike?
- What are my future dreams? How do I feel about them?

After three weeks of effort, notice how your feelings vocabulary has grown. If you are sharing this awareness with a partner, notice how your sense of connection is strengthened.

Expressing Emotions

Emotional injury and healing follow the same patterns as physical injury and healing. As a nurse, I have seen many cases of ill-informed patients with infected wounds they decided merely needed to be covered. Instead of opening the wound to cleanse it and air it out, they applied another bandage or dressing to the seeping area. As the wound inevitably became more and more sore to the touch, the patient's activity would become limited. Eventually we would see the patient in the hospital, because the infection got into the bloodstream and threatened the patient's life. We then had to stabilize the patient, remove all of the dressings, clean the wound and allow all the purulent fluid to drain so that healing could take place and free the patient from pain and limitations. As graphic as it may sound, this is the best analogy I have found to explain what happens to us when we cover up our emotional wounds.

When emotions stay hidden they grow and fester, making dealing with them appear quite frightening. Without proper treatment we become more and more sensitive to issues that remind us unconsciously of our wounds, and sometimes we begin to limit our activities or experiences for fear of more pain. Eventually, our emotional wounds can become so infected that they leak into our life circumstances, destroying relationships or threatening our physical health. However, when we take off the Band-Aids of denial and repression and open up the emotions to expression, we release the emotional "pus pockets" and create a space for emotional healing. Thus, less burdened and limited, we are free to enjoy the emotions we like.

Eventually, you will find that as you embrace your emotions they start to have less of a grip on you. Emotions start to become temporary experiences rather than permanent ways of being, much like the difference between sometimes feeling sad and being a sad person, or the difference between saying "I *have* a pimple" and "I *am* a pimple." The paradox is that the more you allow uncomfortable emotions to exist without expressing them, the more likely it is that you will be negatively impacted by them for extended periods of time. Correspondingly, you will have less time for pleasant emotions such as joy and peace. As you embrace your emotions, they start to have less of a grip on you.

Feelings about Feelings

In adolescence we begin to judge our feelings. Stated another way, we begin to have feelings about our feelings, which compounds our feelings. These *compound feelings* can spiral, becoming more and more uncomfortable, as we add layer upon layer of negative judgments about our feelings. Fortunately, we can learn to decompound our feelings and experience raw feelings without judgment. The capacity to feel our feelings without judgment is an enriching and rewarding experience that can help us find a greater depth within ourselves, and increase our personal intimacy and sense of satisfaction in relationships.

The next time you experience compound feelings, begin to decompound the heap. Take one emotion at a time, starting with the most recent feeling. Acknowledge its right to exist and then release it, without judgment, in order to explore the feeling underneath. When you find the *should*, as in "I *should* feel differently" or "I *shouldn't* feel this way," counter it with permission. Continue this process until you reach the original feeling and nurture it by fulfilling the corresponding need.

Interpreting Emotions

I once had a pet pig named Peggy Suey. I loved Peggy Suey dearly and she taught me many things, including how to relax and live in the moment. One of the most important lessons I learned from her had to do with the challenge of communication.

In the beginning of our relationship, I showed affection to her by patting her head. Unlike my dogs, who loved this kind of attention, she seemed uneasy and would sometimes run away. I was disappointed by her behavior and felt somewhat rebuffed. At other times she would butt her snout into my ankles as if she were angry with me. What made things more confusing was that she did this ankle butting when I thought we were getting along quite well.

Very discouraged and feeling like I had failed to become a healthy "pig parent," I called the woman who had sold Peggy Suey to me. When I described the unusual behavior, she laughed and suggested that I re-read my pig parenting manual. I learned that pigs do not like to be approached from above (as I had done when I patted her head) because, in the baby pig world, predators such as hawks approach from above. Although a pet pig can eventually learn to relax with her caretakers, it takes time; the transition is easier if the pig is approached from under its "chinny-chin-chin." I also learned that ankle butting was Peggy Suey's language for intimacy. So there we were, we cared for each other and yet each of us was confused and distressed by the other's behavior. If I hadn't learned to speak her language she might have ended up as a very expensive ham sandwich!

After further study, I learned that within each and every one of us there exist two languages, corresponding to the two kinds of brains discussed previously. We have a logical, conscious brain (the front brain, cerebral cortex) and an unconscious, emotional brain (the back brain, limbic system). Both brains are intended to help us survive. However, when the communication between the two is poor, we experience discomfort and end up sabotaging ourselves. When the front brain and back brain struggle for power without understanding the value and needs of the other, we are unable to feel peaceful or create the kind of life we want. We can bridge the gap between these two very distinct regions of the brain when the more sophisticated front brain learns the language of the back brain, much as I had to learn Peggy Suey's language because she wasn't sophisticated enough to learn mine. Learning to communicate with the back brain requires understanding the language and logic of emotions. While it may appear that emotions are not logical, they do in fact have a logic of their own. Once emotional blocks are understood, they can become the building blocks for creating a more dynamic and contented life.

As you learn how to interpret your emotions, your decision-making ability will improve. Feelings are an integral part of the decision-making process. On *Star Trek*, Mr. Spock is a very logical, analytical being who is unable to access his feelings. Occasionally, his judgment is impaired when situations involve making "feeling choices" about what is truly appropriate. Feelings not only help make our experiences richer, they also help us in making decisions that are most appropriate or consistent with our value system. Roger, a client of mine who has become very wealthy in the business world, uses a very simple technique. Despite his logical and analytical way of dealing with the world he also has learned to ask himself, "How do I feel about the deal?" If he feels great, it's a deal. If there's any uneasiness, no deal. He reported that his business quadrupled in three years and he saved countless amounts of money by not investing in deals that he did not feel good about, and which he later learned had soured for one reason or another.

Without feelings, we have no personal feedback as to whether or not a decision is good for us. There are case studies that demonstrate that certain brain injuries or brain surgeries leave some people unable to access or experience emotions. The lives of these people often disintegrate because, without emotional feedback, one decision seems as good as another. Because they do not feel bad about wrong choices or uncomfortable about making choices that don't work, they may persist in making decisions that prove ruinous.

When you are clear and current emotionally (not carrying around a lot of unfinished emotional baggage from the back brain pathway), and free from compound emotions, you are able to quiet your mind. This quiet allows you to hear your heart's desire, fulfill your purpose and experience passion as a result.

Talk to friends and determine which aspects of your emotional expression are undeveloped. Become familiar with the positive intentions of your uncomfortable emotions. Then observe at least one incident in another's behavior that demonstrates your understanding of the positive intention of each emotion. Here is an example: today I was at the grocery store and observed a young woman get very angry when told the store would not accept her check. Her baby was crying and she was buying formula and baby food. Since anger is a response to hurt or fear, I bet her anger was a protective reaction to the fear that she might not be able to provide for her child. And if she shops there regularly, she might have felt hurt that the manager wasn't more sympathetic to her needs.

4

The Seven Most Misunderstood Emotions

O nce you understand the positive intention of an emotion and how to express it constructively, emotional blocks can be transformed into building blocks for making your dreams come true. Developing a positive emotional attitude is the foundation for dream-energizing passion. A positive emotional attitude reflects an understanding that emotions are neither right nor wrong. Emotion is energy that mirrors perception (of self and situation). All emotions have a positive intention, including those traditionally thought to be negative, such as anger, grief or jealousy.

Research that has discovered the health benefits of expressing emotions leads me to believe we need to redefine positive and negative emotions. Through personal experience and years of working with clients, I have created a new working definition of positive and negative emotions. *Positive* emotions are those that you can express constructively without harming yourself or others. *Negative* emotions are those that you either do not express, or that you express in destructive ways that harm yourself or others. In short, the expression of the emotion determines whether it is positive or negative. Under this new definition, expressing anger constructively is positive (and healthy) and suppressing joy in the attempt to look cool or in control is negative.

Imprinting Responses

When you judge a feeling to be wrong or inappropriate, you create another uncomfortable feeling in response to your judgment. Have you ever found yourself feeling bad about feeling bad? Feeling guilty about feeling good? Or feeling angry about feeling sad? As if dealing with one feeling isn't enough, you sometimes end up with a cluster of feelings about your feelings. This process of compounding emotions, discussed in chapter 3, results from the brain's capacity for self-awareness, which develops neurologically during the teen years and is what makes teenagers so self-conscious. During adolescence, you develop awareness of the ability to think about thinking and have feelings about feelings, a process that continues throughout adult life. Culturally and socially you are imprinted or conditioned to believe that specific life circumstances should produce a particular type of response (watch that *should* word). If you find yourself feeling something other than what you believe you should feel, you develop uncomfortable feelings about your feelings.

The Intention of Emotions

When an emotion gets compounded by other feelings, the intention of the original emotion gets lost. When you learn how to interpret correctly the original intention of an emotion, not only is your internal experience more pleasant, but you will be guided to find the way to meet your emotional needs. In order to avoid compounding emotions in the first place, it is necessary to give yourself permission to access your emotions, and to honor them by responding to them in a healthy and respectful manner.

Otherwise, you may have to learn the hard way like Lauren, a forty-two-year-old client of mine, who often found herself involved with selfish and rather rough men. She was extremely jealous of her girlfriends who always seemed to have thoughtful and affectionate men in their lives. She found herself feeling guilty about feeling jealous, then feeling angry about feeling guilty, and finally feeling guilty about feeling angry. Talk about emotional dominoes! Lauren followed my instructions on decompounding her emotions. She learned that the positive intention of guilt is to express unexpressed resentment and the positive intention of anger is to identify hurt or fear and express it in a healthy way. As she expressed each layer of feeling, she was able to release it and was finally free to deal with the original emotion of jealousy. Lauren learned that the positive intention of jealousy is to make us aware of those traits in others that we are about to develop. Once Lauren understood each positive intention, she not only stopped feeling guilty about feeling jealous, she actually looked forward to jealousy because she knew that with a little time and effort she was on her way to enjoying the same quality of relationships for herself that she envied in others.

1. Anger

Anger is a protective response to hurt or fear and a signal to let you know that you are not getting what you need. Because anger activates people, it is hailed as a "healing feeling." People can use the fuel of anger to give them the energy to get what they need. In a case of social injustice, for example, anger about the injustice activates people into taking corrective action. Appropriate constructive action is the key to dealing with anger in a healthy way. When expressed constructively, anger can be used to improve your current state of health, your relationships and your work situations. Raging or suppressing anger without sensitivity to its originating cause is unhealthy. Either extreme is downright dangerous, destructive and bad for your health.

When anger is suppressed it becomes distorted. When we judge that our anger is wrong we try to *control* it rather than *feel* it. Because unexpressed anger can only be controlled for so long, it will eventually leak, explode or implode.

Leaking anger is the result of a passive-aggressive imprint.

For a person who is conditioned to be "nice," the thought of being directly angry (and therefore "not nice") is too threatening. These folks find themselves all too often saying yes when they wish they could say no to requests and demands of others. Eventually their resentment and anger builds until it leaks out through passive behavior that makes other people angry. A passive-aggressive person walks through situations as calm as the eye of a hurricane, distressed by all of the anger that surrounds them. Being in the middle of the situation, it is difficult for them to see that the hurricane is their anger, which other people are now expressing for them. Passive-aggressive behaviors include being late, procrastinating, doing a half-hearted job, and so on.

Occasionally, a person with a passive-aggressive pattern can't leak out the anger fast enough and ends up exploding. Direct expressions of anger can be shocking to the passive-aggressive person, who then resolves to do better (have more control) the next time. As the attempts at control become greater, an even stronger force of suppression is needed to keep larger amounts of anger in check. This leads to a vicious cycle of suppression, leaking and angry outbursts.

Other people are conditioned to be aggressive and they habitually express anger without taking time to explore the hurt or fear underneath. People who are trapped in this pattern of expressing explosive anger are referred to as rage-a-holics. They have grown accustomed to the chemical rush that comes from being angry and never address the factors that instigated their anger in the first place. A rage-a-holic is like someone who is constantly bailing water out of their boat while overlooking the need to patch the hole that created the situation in the first place. When it comes to expressing anger it is important to remember to "patch the holes" (of hurt and fear) while "bailing the boat" (expressing pent up anger) so you can enjoy smooth sailing through life.

The opposite of an explosive, outward expression of anger is an implosive inward movement of anger. Imploding anger is a result of chronic repression and can lead to serious states of depression.

Anger can be intimidating to someone who is afraid of his own anger, especially if that person grew up in a family where it was unsafe to express anger for one reason or another. Some people can remember consciously making a decision in childhood never to grow up to be like their angry monster parents. Understanding that either hurt or fear is at the root of anger (it's always one of the two—there are no exceptions to the rule) can help to overcome the discomfort of feeling angry. I don't believe that a healthy happy person wakes up in the morning and says, "Who am I going to hurt today?"

The degree to which a person attempts to hurt or frighten someone else is an indication of the degree to which that person is hurt or frightened. With this understanding, it is easy to see that a very angry person is simply a very hurt or very frightened person; a moderately angry person is a moderately hurt or moderately frightened person, and so forth. Eventually (with a little practice, of course) you will be able to imagine the childlike hurt or fear behind the ranting and raving or ice cold glare of the adult. Naturally, your response to a hurt or frightened child would be gentle and compassionate. In the same way you would approach a vulnerable child, you will ultimately be able to approach an angry adult without being intimidated or upset yourself. As a result of being less upset yourself you will find that you spend much less time in confrontational situations and more time exploring the underlying reason for the angry response.

When you find yourself feeling angry with someone who doesn't understand the nature of anger, you will have to be responsible for sharing your underlying feelings of hurt or fear, because the person you are upset with won't have a clue as to the origin of your anger.

Expressing anger without sharing the underlying hurt or fear creates a cornered experience for the person at the other end of your anger. If you back an animal into a corner, it will come out biting; if you back a person into a corner, he'll come out fighting. Sharing your hurt or fear not only saves emotional wear and tear but may also save face, as in the case of Paula, a fifty-three-year-old woman and mother of three. A few years ago Paula came to me in tears because her husband had forgotten her birthday for the second year in a row. In fact, the day she saw me was her birthday, and she had received no special card or acknowledgment. She desperately wanted to avoid creating a scene, yet she found herself feeling angry and incredulous. She couldn't imagine he would have forgotten again after last year's horrible experience in which she called him an irresponsible, selfish jerk and they fought for two weeks. Instead of approaching her husband from anger, which in her case would have included yelling and name calling, I suggested that she explain how hurt she felt.

That evening, instead of hurling insults at her husband, Paula calmly explained her feelings of hurt to him. He seemed sincerely remorseful and apologized, saying he obviously didn't realize how important her birthday was to her. He suggested that he make it up to her by taking her out to dinner that night. When they arrived at the restaurant they were greeted by forty of her closest friends for her surprise birthday party. The entire event had been arranged by her wonderful husband! Paula was quite pleased with herself for having chosen to express her hurt rather than attacking in anger; otherwise she might have been eating crow instead of birthday cake.

Coping with Anger

The next time you are angry use the following strategy and notice how much more effective you feel:

- When you find yourself feeling angry find an appropriate place to privately release your anger.
- Use substitute acting-out (for example, yell, scream, kick, run, hit a pillow with a tennis racket) without putting yourself at physical risk.
- Identify the fear or hurt underneath.
- Take constructive action to meet your needs, such as comforting yourself, calling someone who will comfort you, changing your attitude, sharing your hurt or fear with the person with whom you are upset, or ending an unsatisfying relationship.

2. Depression

If anger is not expressed for a long time, a person may become depressed. In fact, depression has been described as anger turned inward. Depression is a very immobilizing experience. The positive intention of this emotion is to protect you. When you are preoccupied with unresolved issues you are not very alert. Immobilization keeps you cocooned and out of harm's way while you gather your resources to deal with whatever losses or traumas have occurred. Cocooning, which can be a healing time to regroup, can also be taken to an extreme, where even the simplest activities of daily living, like eating or getting out of bed, become burdensome and can seem overwhelming.

The antidote to this straightforward type of depression is reversing the direction of anger, which entails expressing anger verbally and maybe even physically. The most dramatic case of depression and its reversal I have witnessed was with Rhonda, a seamstress in her early forties, a very timid and soft-spoken woman, who often found herself victimized by life's circumstances. A few years ago she was diagnosed with terminal cancer. She had just returned from a well-known cancer institute where she was told her situation was hopeless. By this time, she had lost all color in her complexion and no longer had even a hint of her old fighting spirit. She was so weak and depressed that she could barely lift her head from the pillow. She called me to ask if I would do her a favor and find some type of medication to end her life.

I told her that I did not intuitively sense that this was her time to die and asked that she take a little more time to reconsider. As I was leaving her home, I overheard her caretaker say, "It's not the cancer that's killin' her, it's not even the chemo." Because I have learned to listen to wisdom from unexpected sources, I stepped back into the house to hear what this non-therapist, nonprofessional lay person had to say about what Rhonda might need from counseling sessions. I asked the woman to continue. She went on, "Nope, it's not even the bad news that got her down, I tell you. It's the anger with her parents that's choking out the very life of her." I happened to know that Rhonda had serious and long-standing abandonment issues with her parents, but I had always thought we would address those issues if and when she recovered and had the energy to do so.

Involving her parents seemed to me like a long shot, because Rhonda could barely speak and had so little energy; but there was little hope left otherwise and I didn't have a better idea. With Rhonda's permission I flew her parents in to see her. They had always been somewhat intimidating to her. I intervened by asking her parents to sit quietly and listen to Rhonda while she expressed all of the hurt and pain she had experienced during her years of growing up. I asked her parents to avoid defending their position and to simply do the best they could to understand Rhonda's point of view.

At first, Rhonda was quite timid. She apologized profusely and stumbled and bumbled through her sentences. With a little coaching from me and permission from her parents, she began to vent all of the unexpressed anger she had held in for most of her life. Midway through her discourse, I noticed that her face was beginning to get flushed. She sat up straighter and her voice became stronger. By the end of the session, after many tears, Rhonda and her parents had asked for each other's forgiveness for the misunderstandings that had occurred throughout the years. Despite Rhonda's previous weakness and depression, the color never left her face, she began to recover miraculously, and she is now no longer victimized by life. To this day, she is an inspiration to many.

It is important to know that not all depression is caused by an implosion of anger. Like diabetics who have an insufficient amount of the protein insulin, some people have biochemical insufficiencies that make them prone to depression. It is best to seek the help of a qualified professional who can help to determine a physiological versus mental origin for depression.

Coping with Depression

The next time you are feeling depressed:

- Even though you won't feel like it (believe me, I know this is a tough one), find your fighting spirit and resolve to take action by expressing anger. Or use your anger as fuel to make your life or someone else's life better.

• If you have more than two immobilizing bouts of depression a year, have yourself checked for hypoglycemia, which often mimics depression. If depression persists consult a professional for an accurate diagnosis.

3. Fear

Fear is a natural response to the unknown and should be considered a yellow light, alerting you to proceed with caution. The positive intention of fear is to prepare your body for fight or flight when faced with a new or stressful situation. The fight-or-flight response involves gearing up your body for action. Your heart begins to beat faster, your blood pressure increases, and you may experience a dry mouth, perspiration and a sense of tension or edginess. Although the symptoms can be decidedly inconvenient (for example, when preparing to speak in front of a group), the process, if not overwhelming, helps you think more quickly and clearly and keeps you alert and ready to respond. The distortion of fear occurs when you interpret fear or apprehension as a red light directing you to stop moving along your personal path of experience.

Fear can be a helpful friend, not a reason to stop your endeavors. The paradox of fear is that when you stop being afraid of it, you become less frightened. By embracing fear, you lower the emotional stakes. When you lower that narrow balance beam from ten feet in the air, where you could get seriously hurt, to a height of one or two feet, where you might get a little bumped and bruised if a fall occurred at all, you can more easily fulfill your dreams.

Fear can have a paralyzing effect in every area of life, and as the paralysis spreads, self-esteem begins to dwindle. As self-esteem decreases, the way out of the fearful situation seems less and less possible. Mary Ann was an example of this type of cyclical thinking. She was forty-nine years old when I first met her. She came to see me for help with feelings of anxiety and bouts of depression. Mary Ann, by most people's standards, was quite successful. She had three grown and self-sufficient children. She worked as a nurse in a psychiatric unit, which was her favorite kind of nursing. She owned a home and was in a healthy relationship with a man she would ultimately marry.

The problem was, she wasn't happy. Her career, which had seemed so satisfying years ago, now bored her to tears. She longed to continue psychiatric nursing but in a different setting. Every time she considered making a change, however, she was gripped by fear. She interpreted her fear as a signal that she wasn't ready to take the risk of seeking out more satisfactory employment. After three months of gentle prompting and encouragement, she finally took the leap of faith and quit her job to become a school nurse. Here is an excerpt from a thank-you letter she sent me:

> *Dear Tina,*
>
> *I am now working as a school nurse, making the same amount of money per year with better hours, no shift work, holidays and three months off! I love the mix of blending routine treatment with counseling. This is the perfect job for me. I want to thank you for encouraging me to follow my heart and pushing me off of that cliff, which when I look back was only a foot high!*
>
> *Love,*
> *Mary Ann*

If you find that you are crippled by a self-limiting response to fear, read "Permission to Be Less Than Perfect," chapter 7, and do the exercises.

4. Jealousy

Jealousy is a result of seeing unowned positive aspects of oneself in another. It is an indicator of potential growth. The purpose of jealousy is to encourage you to develop unowned aspects within yourself. Jealousy is an indication of what you are about to do, become, or have if you cultivate a given attribute. Jealousy has gotten bad press ever since envy was described as one of the Seven Deadly Sins by Saint Thomas Aquinas. It's not jealousy that is the problem but the distortion that is destructive and unhealthy.

Just watch how children grow and become more proficient. If a child sees another child who is riding a bike, tying a shoe, or learning how to tell time, the child thinks, "Oh, I want to do that," and sets about learning how to acquire those skills. The distortion of jealousy occurs when, rather than identifying elements we would like to learn or become, we belittle someone's talent or good fortune or wish them harm. How stunted would a child be if every time she saw a skill she found useful she said to herself, "Who does that boy think he is? He's showing off just because he can ride a bike. I never wanted to learn how to ride a bike anyway," or "Those shoestrings are ugly. I'd rather have Velcro than learn how to tie my shoes."

I remember the first time I dealt with my jealousy in a positive way. I was at the house of a friend who was hosting a party. You may not believe this, but I am rather shy and the idea of hosting a party had always been uncomfortable to me. I was very impressed by this hostess, who not only looked great, but was as cool as a cucumber. It was a perfect party. The perfect number of people showed up. The perfect music was playing. Everything was perfect. I found myself feeling perfectly jealous. I wished her soufflé would flop or her dress would tear or that something would just go wrong. The more I imagined potential party disasters and my delight at the thought of an actual occurrence, the more uncomfortable I became. I realized I was making myself miserable and not benefiting in the least from this way of thinking. When I considered that my jealousy was an indication that I might have a growing interest in learning how to be more sociable, I laughed. No way, not me, I'm not a society girl. And yet, I trusted that I wouldn't be having this feeling if some part of me wasn't welling up inside of me and preparing to express itself.

I went up to Ms. Perfect Hostess and asked her if she could tell me how she created such a wonderful party yet remained so calm and cool. Her response? She said, "Are you kidding? My family thinks I am a *maniac* for a week." "Oh really," I smiled. "Yes," she said, "I drive them crazy." I breathed a sigh of relief, saying, "Really? Tell me all about it." She went on to explain all of the secrets of hosting a great party, such as the party formula: Multiply the number of people you invite by 0.75; with good weather, that's how many will attend. Subtract ten percent for bad weather. (Who ever would have thought?) She even gave me the recipe for her soufflé: the corner bakery (Hey, I could do that!). Three months later, I gave the best party I had ever been to and really enjoyed myself. From then on, I was no longer jealous of Ms. Hostess with the Mostest because I had cultivated within myself the traits of a great hostess. From then on, we were both great hostesses and much better friends.

Now that I understand jealousy, I look forward to being jealous. In fact, I have a friend in the National Speakers Association who is my jealousy buddy. He tells me about his accomplishments until I turn a dark shade of envy green. When I'm good and jealous, he'll say, "Great, because that is what you are about to become!" Later, I'll call him up and tell him how his success spurred me on to greater success of my own. We encourage one another, leapfrogging over each other's successes to become more of what we are meant to become.

Some people have difficulty owning their jealousy because they see it as ungrateful or an indication that they are not appreciating the gifts that God has given them. I believe that jealousy is God's way of letting you know what gifts you already have that you have not yet developed. Jealousy is the indicator of the spiritual self emerging and gives you a guidepost for where you are headed.

If you ignore or deny jealousy you will continue to be annoyed and aggravated by other people's successes, qualities or attributes. You may find yourself belittling the attributes that you are jealous of but doing little to further your own progress.

Knocking the other person has a stifling effect and keeps you from cultivating the very quality that you desire.

When attempting to discern your jealousy, it is helpful to look for the elements of your jealousy. For instance, many people are jealous of movie stars but it doesn't necessarily mean that they want to become movie stars. For some people, the elements of being a star that may be appealing are financial freedom, the ability to make a difference in the world, or the accolades and recognition of talent that attend stardom. Once you can identify the element and cultivate it, you can claim it as your own. I want to remind you that it is impossible to be jealous of another if that element is not in some form or another already a part of you just waiting to be expressed.

I once had a client who had a very strong negative reaction to my definition of jealousy. Jerome was paraplegic and had been in a wheelchair for most of his life. He said that he had worked hard not to be jealous of people. To him, jealousy was a destructive feeling because he always felt jealous of people who could walk, but it was impossible for him to cultivate this ability. In searching for the elements of his jealousy, I asked him, "What is it about people walking that makes you feel jealous?" He said, "Obviously, I am jealous because people can move faster than I can. They can get from one place to another more quickly." I asked him if he thought it was possible that the element of *movement* was what he was jealous of, more than getting from one place to another physically.

At first, this was a confusing concept to Jerome, but as we talked about his ability to change or move internally, he realized that he had always had a difficult time letting go of old ideas and old ways of being. He observed that his internal growth was always relatively slow compared to others. As he learned how to more easily embrace the concept of change, he began to create important personal changes in his attitude and choices in living. Although it would always be his preference to be able to walk, he no longer felt jealous of people who moved quickly, because he was now one of them.

Coping with Jealousy

The next time you find yourself feeling jealous:

- Notice any tendency within yourself to belittle the person or situation that makes you feel jealous.
- Make an agreement with yourself to focus on the positive intention of jealousy and use your feeling of animosity as a benchmark to indicate your progress in claiming your unowned aspects. In other words, pay attention to your upset feeling only as a measure of how close or far away you are from cultivating that quality you are about to acquire. (Lots of upset—you're far away. A little upset—getting closer. No upset whatsoever—almost there! Feeling admiration—Bingo!)
- Identify the elements that are causing you to feel jealous by asking yourself, "What exactly about this person or this person's situation do I want? If I had what this person has, how would my life be different?"
- Once the element is identified, ask yourself, "How can I create that quality or aspect in my life?"
- Take action steps to create the desired quality.
- When you find yourself not only feeling neutral but admiring your former nemesis, you know you have arrived.
- Time to be on the lookout for your next episode of jealousy, which will point the way to your next journey of growth!

5. Guilt

Guilt is initially a social learning tool that allows you to know when you trespass on your own integrity or violate your values. Healthy guilt is very useful as a "self-correcting" emotion. For the first fifteen minutes you experience guilt, it teaches you that you have violated your own value system. If, however, guilt persists after self-corrections are applied, which usually takes about fifteen minutes, it moves out of the range of healthy and becomes distorted and toxic. Guilt that persists after a lesson is learned is not actually guilt at all but is unexpressed resentment masquerading as guilt.

Unhealthy guilt is always fueled by an unhealthy, unrealistic and distorted moral imperative. Take the case of Tom, a forty-five-year-old business executive who owned a successful and somewhat demanding business. Tom was a single parent to three children, and had siblings and aging parents who were always asking for more of his time than he could comfortably give. He was plagued with enormous feelings of guilt because he thought he should be visiting his parents more often. When I asked him, "Is it possible that you might be feeling a little resentment?" his response was, "No, not me. I just feel bad because I should be visiting my parents more often."

"Well then," I suggested, "what if you just *imagined* that you were resentful? If you pretended to feel resentful, what might it be related to?" He thought briefly. "Let's see, *if* I were resentful, it *might* be because my parents always call on me and not my five brothers and sisters when they need something. Or it might be because they didn't get a life, and they are always looking to me to entertain them." He continued, his face getting tighter and more pained. "They're always depending on me! Why does it always have to be me?" The next thing I knew he was no longer pretending. He was truly experiencing resentment. I asked him if he felt any guilt while he was in the middle of his resentful state. "Absolutely not."

It is impossible to feel guilt and resentment at the same time in the same way that it is impossible to simultaneously feel joy and anger. I encouraged him to stay with his feelings of resentment and give the benefit of the doubt to all concerned with the situation. The more he discussed the situation, the more he realized that his parents were doing the best they could. In the era in which they had been raised, it wasn't the right thing to do for seniors to take care of themselves. They hadn't been taught that happiness and fulfillment come from within. They had been taught to put others first and expect that eventually others would anticipate and fulfill their needs.

As Tom considered their history and lack of resources, he began to feel compassion. He was able to forgive them for being human. His guilt-ridden *should* was transformed into a freeing *could.* Thereafter, whenever he visited his parents, he really enjoyed being with them. And though he neither increased the frequency of visits nor the amount of time with his parents, they reported that he stayed longer and visited more often than he actually did! I suspect that the reason they perceived his visits as longer and more frequent was because his visits now were made by his free choice; therefore, he was truly present. All of his attention was focused on his parents rather than watching the TV or his watch and wishing his time was up. Other than an occasional guilt pang, which is warranted when he violates his integrity, Tom reports that he is totally free of "toxic guilt."

Coping with Guilt

The next time you find yourself feeling guilt:

- Ask yourself if you have violated your sense of values. For example, you may find that you don't feel good about telling a "little white lie" or behaving in an inappropriate manner.
- If you have violated your values, learn from this experience and vow to make amends and/or handle the situation differently in the future. You will feel a sense of relief if you are accurate.
- If feelings of guilt persist for more than fifteen minutes after you have identified the source of guilt and have learned from the situation, explore a possible source of resentment related to the situation (hint: look for the should).
- Immerse yourself fully in the feeling of resentment.
- To determine whether you are embracing resentment, ask yourself if you feel guilt. If you still feel guilt, it is an indication that you are not fully immersed in resentment.
- When you are feeling totally righteous in the middle of your resentment, give all persons involved, including yourself, the benefit of the doubt. If you do this sincerely, you will notice a sense of compassion developing.
- Before you know it, your should will be replaced by a could and that is the end of unhealthy guilt.

6. Sadness

Sadness is welcomed as a cleansing emotion, which says goodbye to changing situations and people. When embraced, it allows for completion of unfinished emotional issues. Sadness allows for new beginnings. If left unfinished for too long, sadness becomes distorted. Chronic sadness can be exhausting and detrimental to your health and well-being. Our culture avoids sadness and does not tolerate vulnerability. Sadness is often associated with weakness. How many times have you heard that someone is "handling a loss well"? This means they haven't broken down or lost it by crying or expressing sadness. It is much easier (especially for men in our society) to feel rage or create upset around sadness than to feel vulnerable. Because sadness is not a pleasant feeling to experience, we tend to try to push it down or repress it. Chronic sadness, like all uncomfortable feelings, results in feeling much worse than you would have had you allowed yourself to feel total and acute sadness and then moved through it.

One of the real dangers of holding onto chronic sadness is that you can become victimized by not balancing sadness with anger (remember, anger initiates action.) Feeling sad constantly, without taking action to change either your perception of the situation or the situation itself, leads to a perpetual state of victimization. Another danger of not dealing with sadness effectively is that you may avoid situations and relationships that could end in sadness. And because every situation or relationship will eventually have some sadness associated with it, opportunities for growth and happiness are avoided.

The most important step in dealing with sadness is to say goodbye. Goodbye is one of the most difficult words for people in our culture to use. Saying goodbye to situations makes real the change and loss associated with them. Many people fear that saying goodbye will cause them to be so flooded with sadness that they will never get out from under it. Paradoxically, the opposite is true. If you dam up your feelings you risk drowning in a sea of sadness. But if you embrace your sadness and feel it acutely, you ultimately have to deal with less sadness. As you pay attention to your feelings, you will notice that sadness has a wave-like action. The first waves may seem unbearable, but when embraced, they eventually become less intense and are replaced by peace.

Long periods of sadness can lead a person to become depersonalized. In this state, the victimization process destroys self-esteem and leaves the person feeling worthless, unloved, and not in control of his or her life's circumstances. This happened to a former client of mine named Pamela, a woman in her midfifties and mother of three grown children. Pamela came to see me because she was being treated for cancer and was having severe side effects from chemotherapy. From her comments, it seemed to me that she perceived chemotherapy as something she had to do and thought her treatment was beyond her control. She casually remarked that this situation reminded her of a time thirty years before when she delivered a stillborn child and it was as if her body was no longer hers. At that time, she was told to go home and pretend that these traumatic events hadn't happened. She had not been allowed to touch the child or grieve for the child. Her doctor even suggested that she "hurry up and get pregnant so you will forget about this one." I sensed intuitively that she had not grieved for her unborn child.

One week later, Pamela, her husband and I went to the graveyard where her stillborn child had been buried. She brought flowers and named him and grieved intensely for a child who would have been thirty years old had he lived. After that experience, she began an incredible healing journey, which included seeing herself again as a person who was capable of influencing her life's circumstances. She not only completed her course of chemotherapy with much less fear and fewer side effects, but she went on to help others in need of encouragement and support during their trials and tribulations. Saying goodbye to the past allowed her to say hello to the present moment and empowered her to move forward into her future.

I have worked with many people who have not said goodbye and experienced the sadness associated with the loss of a loved one, a marriage or a job. Whenever I ask someone whether they have said goodbye and the response is "I think I have" or "I'm not sure," then I know they haven't. If you have to guess whether you said goodbye, the answer is no. There is a definite knowledge of when one has grieved over a loss that makes room for new life. I have noticed that families who say goodbye to a loved one during the dying process consistently heal much more quickly and fully than people who do not express their sadness.

Sadness is often confused with depression. Sadness has a heavy, weighted quality about it. It may slow us down enough to feel our pain so that we can release it, but unlike depression, it is not immobilizing.

Coping with Loss

The next time you suffer a loss:

- Identify the loss clearly. For example, the sadness that results from the loss of a job may actually be related to loss of security, loss of income, or loss of connection to the people at work.
- List all of your appreciations and resentments associated with the person or situation before the loss was experienced.
- Say "Goodbye (name of the person or situation)" and state a resentment related to that person or situation. Follow with "Goodbye (name of the person or situation)" and state an appreciation related to that person or situation. Do this until you have described all of your resentments and appreciations. (Don't kid yourself into thinking that you don't have any appreciations. If you didn't have any appreciations, you wouldn't feel sad in the first place.)
- Allow yourself to cry freely. If you have difficulty with this, see a therapist or counselor for assistance.
- Repeat step 3 until your process is complete. (This could take months depending on the situation. Sadness that interferes with the ability to experience any happiness during the grieving process is considered serious and needs professional help.)

7. Joy

The feeling of joy lets you know that you are living "on purpose." That is, you are living a life that honors and expresses your original self. Discovering your purpose is a tricky business at times because the road to self-discovery is fraught with many misconceptions.

I remember a discussion in my first-grade religion class in which our teacher spoke to us about discovering our life's purpose. According to my teacher, God gave me my body and I was created to know, love and serve him. One day, she said, when I became an adult, God would speak to me and reveal my purpose. In doing so, he would tell me how I could best serve him. If I answered "the call," I would know unspeakable happiness. But if I didn't, I would forever be lost, possibly live a life of sin and suffer eternal damnation.

I remember feeling a little nervous. Because I wanted to be a saint when I grew up, I hoped that God would see me as decent saintly material and consider me for the job. However, I figured that to become a saint would require taking on a grueling job, like being a missionary in a foreign country. I was an extremely finicky eater as a child and I worried about how I would eat the natives' food. I was also concerned about how much I would miss my parents if I had to live far away. While I hoped God had a purpose in mind for me, I feared I wouldn't be able to live up to the job and would be miserable in the process.

Later, as an adult, when I no longer considered myself religious (and being a saint was the last thing I qualified for), I made an incredible discovery. Every time I used my God-given talents to do what I liked to do, I grew as a person, clients were healed, and I experienced joy. What a relief it was for me to learn that experiencing joy is an indication of whether or not I am on purpose. When I feel passionately joyful, there is no question that I am doing the right work or have chosen the right type of vocation, relationship, lifestyle, whatever. Although I now work much harder and more intensely than I ever did when doing work that didn't utilize my potential, I rarely complain. When I am on purpose, I am fully immersed and extremely passionate. What I do and who I am merges into an almost timeless space. It is in this space that I feel extremely creative and inspired. I experience the place that athletes call "the zone" or "being in the flow." Even though the task may be difficult or challenging, total absorption and intensity allows me to get out of my own way and become a channel for the passionate expression of my original self.

In my Gestalt training, I learned that as many people suffer from repressed joy as suffer from repressed anger, hurt, guilt, and so forth. At first, I found this a rather absurd concept to accept. Yet after years of experience, I have witnessed many times when people do, in fact, suppress joy. The reasons are many but all boil down to fear. The three main fears are fear of looking foolish, fear of being out of control and fear of being disappointed.

Let's take a quick look at these three joy-distorting fears.

1. *Fear of looking foolish.* This fear is due to childhood imprints that tell you that once you become an adult, you must look and act mature and responsible. What they forgot to tell you when you were growing up is that you will always feel like a child on the inside, especially when joy arises. For the record: A mature adult knows herself well and has grown beyond living up (or down) to the expectations of others. Maturity means being truthful with oneself and honoring the essence of one's soul and its expression. A responsible adult is able to respond to her internal states and gives herself permission to freely express any emotion, including joy, in a healthy, constructive manner.

2. *Fear of being out of control.* Ever try to have an orgasm and stay in control? Need I say more?

3. *Fear of disappointment.* I often hear people say things like "I'm afraid of feeling too happy or joyful because I just know something bad will happen" or "I can't relax and enjoy myself because I know I'll be disappointed when the good time is over" or "I find myself just waiting for the other shoe to fall." I wonder if you've noticed that pleasant events follow unpleasant events just about as often as unpleasant events follow pleasant ones. It is the

cyclic nature of life. Disappointing things will not happen because you feel good, but because the rhythm of life is up and down, dark and light, birth and death, ebb and flow, on and on. It's best to enjoy joy while it's here. Otherwise, you won't even be able to enjoy a good meal, because sooner than later it will be over!

Even though someone may not have verbalized specifically what their purpose is, most of us can easily discover our purpose by paying attention to those events and situations in our life that make us feel very alive, full and satisfied. Purpose is not so much what you do but how you do what you do; that is, how you weave your unique gifts, talents and interests into whatever activity you participate in. For example, I have always enjoyed being a teacher. As a child, I liked to come home and play "school" with my neighborhood friends almost every day after school. I guess I must have really liked being a teacher, because one of my earliest memories is of my mom calling me in from the front porch of our home and saying, "Tina, you can't always be the teacher; be sure to let your friends have their turn too." When I became an adult, I majored in elementary education but became disillusioned with our educational system and decided that perhaps I was not really meant to be a teacher after all. I went into nursing, but found myself gravitating toward the patient education aspects of nursing. Later, as a social worker, I discovered that what I enjoyed most was (you guessed it) teaching clients empowerment.

When I realized that teaching is part of my purpose, I looked back over my life and saw that teaching had been an inextricable element of my life regardless of what formal role I played at a given time. My mother's words followed me into adulthood. I learned that even though I was now getting paid to teach, I couldn't always be the teacher. Learning from listening to others has made me a much better life student and ultimately a better teacher as well.

For some people, simply identifying one's purpose is enough to get focused and begin living a purposeful and passionate life. For others, even when the purpose has been identified, there may be resistance to living it. The greatest fear most people come up against in the process of expressing their purpose is fear of rejection. This archaic fear is rooted in the fear of abandonment we all experience as children. A child abandoned during the early years of life would more than likely perish. On an unconscious level (limbic system imprinting), human beings are conditioned to "fit in" for fear of being left out to perish on their own. We forget that we are adults capable of taking care of ourselves. And even though the fear may be experienced as real, when we look behind the curtain, we'll see that there is little to be afraid of. Although as adults we can survive physical abandonment, our spiritual health cannot survive the abandonment of our purpose.

Pam, a friend of mine, grew up with the dream of being a beautician. When she was a child and later, in early adulthood, she could think of nothing that she enjoyed more than playing with makeup and hair colors to enhance personal appearance. When it was time to make a career choice, however, she opted to become a paralegal instead of a beautician. She thought a paralegal would have more status and earn greater respect in the world's view (which she later realized was a projection of her parents' point of view). For many long years she was an excellent paralegal but a miserable person. The death of her husband led her to re-evaluate her situation. She realized that her fear of her family's criticism and rejection of her values was what had kept her from doing what she wanted to do most. Then it occurred to her that the worst rejection of all was self-rejection. She realized she was rejecting her own values and desires. She immediately decided it was time to create her life in a purposeful and meaningful way.

Although somewhat apprehensive at first, she quit her job as a paralegal and went to beauty school. She then created a business designed to teach women how to enhance both their physical and inner beauty. While discussing makeup and trying different wardrobe colors, Pam reminds her clients that the most important foundation (no pun intended) for their beauty is loving themselves and being true to their purpose. Her clients are happier than ever and, most importantly, so is she. Pam says, "When I look back, I see how easy it was to ignore my yearnings for the sake of fitting in with my family and friends. But what a price I paid. I now wake up every day excited about what the day will bring. I know I'm making a difference in others' lives. Even though I work hard, it feels like play. I am so grateful for the forces in my life that helped me to listen to and follow the call of my life purpose."

There is a term for giving up one's purpose and sacrificing authenticity. It is called codependency. If you are unfamiliar with the term, here is one definition: Codependency is when you have a near-death experience and someone else's life flashes before your eyes! It is when you give up your will and the expression of who you genuinely are for another person, or an organization. In some ways, it is comforting to join forces with others and lose your identity in the process as part of a couple or a group. That's part of the "safety in numbers" syndrome. But the price can be rather steep. People in your life who ask (or demand) that you not be authentically who you are and who do not support your purpose have not yet learned how to love unconditionally. Unconditional love requires that we allow those we love to express their uniqueness and encourage them to follow the path of their heart's desire. Unconditional love never threatens, rules, manipulates, or in any way attempts to hinder another's freedom and right to become who they are meant to become. Unconditional love supports authenticity and promotes joy.

When we release our expectations of ourselves— expectations of who and what we think we should be—and allow ourselves to be drawn to that which inspires and expresses our essence, we are more able to hear and follow our purpose. When we get "off purpose," we will experience a restlessness characterized by a sense that something is missing, even though by the world's standards, and perhaps by our own standards, we are living a good life. Restlessness alerts us to an internal shift. While yesterday's pace of life may have seemed restful, today the very same pace may be dull and boring. Or although yesterday's work seemed exciting, today it seems chaotic and overwhelming or even uninteresting. The tendency for many of us is to ignore the changes that occur internally. After all, if life was fine last week, we don't even stop to consider that somehow we may have changed inside and our growing sense of who we are is calling out for a change in our circumstances to meet our needs. My experience has proven to me on countless occasions that when I answer this call and take action to transform the restlessness to peace, I return to an ever higher sense of purpose and joy. Not every bit of restlessness calls for a major life change. Sometimes subtle pangs of a need to change can help us adjust our current life situation to make it more satisfying.

For example, when I was first hired as an RN at a psychiatric hospital, I was elated. I couldn't believe I was actually getting paid to do something I loved so much. As I became proficient at my new job, I didn't feel as challenged. I noticed I lost a little enthusiasm. I became more comfortable than passionate. I began experiencing restlessness as I listened to patients talking about their problems, and my eyes would wander to the huge picture windows overlooking the levee of the Mississippi River. I felt envious of the people jogging on the levee. Now that I had mastered the mental components of my work I missed having a physical element. "How can I alter my job to include the work I like to do and also be able to jog?" I asked myself. I decided to create a stress management and jogging program. Creating it was fun and taking the risk to present it was exciting. Honoring my divine restlessness brought me back to feeling passionate about my work. And, of course, getting paid for it and seeing patients become healthier was quite a reward!

An added benefit to living "on purpose" is increased physical health. People who are living passionately and on purpose suffer from fewer colds and minor illnesses. In cases of more serious illness people who live on purpose generally respond more favorably to treatment than their less purposeful counterparts. On-purpose people who are dying experience more peace and leave their families with less unfinished emotional wreckage after their deaths, because on-purpose people live so fully that they have few regrets and they know that in whatever amount of time they had on this earth, they truly lived. Live passionately, die peacefully. In my experience with dying people, I have come to the conclusion that the tragedy in life is not dying, but is having failed to live an authentic and purposeful life.

Living with Joy

For more joy:

- Ask yourself and a few close friends or family members to describe your special gifts, talents and interests. Begin your plan to incorporate as many of these as possible into creating and living your life purpose.
- Write a list of the things you do and the ways you think that bring you joy. For one week, as you go through your usual routine, ask yourself how you can weave each aspect of joy into your moment-to-moment living in all of your life circumstances.

5

Power

Power: the ability to create yourself as the kind of person you want to be and to create whatever kind of life you want.

Creating the Life That Supports Your Peace and Passion

True power is an internal experience that results in the ability to create yourself as the kind of person you want to be and to create whatever kind of life you want. True power is not determined by external circumstances such as money, position in society or the kind of car you drive. Power based on those external circumstances lasts only as long as the circumstances are present. As soon as the money is gone, the position is lost or the car is demolished, so goes that kind of power. True power is internal and constant and does not diminish in relationship to anything or anyone outside of you. Power is not to be confused with control. Controlling others in order to do or be what you want them to do or be is domination and not a reflection of personal power.

Power can be measured by your ability to manifest. To manifest is to make real or create. It involves taking the abstract world of thought and imagination and giving it concrete shape and form. As your power increases, your ability to manifest increases. You will find that as you become more powerful you will be able to manifest increasingly more complex dreams with less effort and often in less time.

The process of building personal power is very similar to that of building physical strength. To get stronger physically, one must start with lifting a small amount of weight repetitively and consistently until that weight is easy to manage. As the muscles respond by getting larger and stronger, the amount of weight is gradually increased. Building "manifestation muscles" is no different. The secret of building manifestation muscles is simple, but not always easy. The key to becoming an increasingly more powerful person is *clarity*. Clarity means being free from confusion, ambivalence, uncertainty, or any degree of cloudiness in your thoughts and actions.

There are five main areas of your life in which clarity is essential in order to manifest swiftly and accurately. To be the most powerful person possible you need:

- Clarity in your mental and emotional life
- Clarity in your desires
- Clarity in your actions
- Clarity in your intuition
- Clarity in relationship to a power greater than yourself

Let's investigate each of these areas to make sure that you are as clear, and therefore as powerful, as possible.

Clarity in Your Mental and Emotional Life

If you practice the principles of peace and passion with any regularity you will automatically evolve into a more compassionate and emotionally healthier person. As your mental and emotional world becomes clearer and lighter, limiting imprints and beliefs weaken and your ability to create a life to suit your special needs improves dramatically.

The danger of developing the ability to manifest without working through mental and emotional issues beforehand is that the issues *themselves* become filters through which you manifest. For example, if you have an imprint that suggests that you are weak or limited in some way, your personal power will energize that belief and prove you right. The irony is that the stronger your personal power is, the weaker and more limited you will become. Or suppose you have an imprint that says you do not deserve wealth, or health, or love. Your uncertainty and mixed emotions about these issues will then create uncertain and mixed results. However, if your mental and emotional intentions are clear and focused, your results will be clear and focused too.

Clarity in Your Desires

If you were to hop into a cab in a new city and tell the driver, "I want to get somewhere sometime today," it is likely that you would never reach your destination. One thing is for certain. You would have spent a lot less time and money had you gotten into the cab and given the directions, "Please take me to Forty-first and Main Street. I would like to be there in twenty minutes, if possible, so please take the simplest and fastest way." Likewise, when we clearly know what we want (our goal) and energize it with emotion, we activate our brain to go into hunter mode and we become sensitive to opportunities that can lead to the fulfillment of our dreams. (Exactly how this is done is explained in chapter 6, "Training the Brain.")

In nursing school, I learned that in order to be effective, goals must be objective, measurable and realistic. It wasn't enough to say "The patient will walk more." My instructors insisted that my goals be objective, observable and measurable, therefore a more specific goal is "The patient will walk twenty feet to the nurses' station." Anyone could have stood in my place, observed the patient walking and measured the distance.

The more specific and detailed the goal, the easier it will be to reel it in. Here are some examples of general goals versus specific goals that are objective and measurable:

General Goals	Specific Goals
I'd like to have more money	I will earn $750 per week
I'd like to be in better physical shape	I will jog two miles each day
I'd like to improve my grades	I'm going to get at least a 3.2 average this fall

When it comes to goals, there are two things I didn't learn in nursing school that are very important to know in life: 1) Not all goals need to be realistic; and 2) The goal can seem impossible, but the steps needed to get there must be realistic.

In creating goals, ask yourself questions that help you determine if your life situation is meeting your needs in a healthy manner. Is your lifestyle becoming more of an expression of your passion every day? Is the way you are living promoting more peace in your life? What needs to stay the same? What needs to change? You may want to take a few minutes now to review your life. Make sure that you are surrounding yourself with an environment that supports and nourishes your sense of peace and need for passion.

Suggested areas to explore include:

- House/home
- Loved ones
- Friends
- Pets
- Community
- Spiritual life
- Food
- Exercise
- Recreational activities
- Books
- Learning opportunities
- Music
- Time alone

After reviewing the above areas and any other areas of your life that are important to you, write down next to each one what action needs to be taken. Write down what keeps you from taking the necessary steps you know you need to take. Review the next section on clarity and follow through.

Clarity in Action

One of the most common pitfalls I see in failure to manifest dreams is lack of action. Did you ever hear the one about ol' Jon

Boudreaux? Well, a while back, and some time ago, ol' Jon Boudreaux, who lived down on the bayou, was down on his luck and unable to provide financially for his family. The shrimping and crabbing season was the worst ever and he was some worried. Well, ol' Boudreaux, he begged God to allow him to win the lottery so he could take care of his family, and promised in return to dedicate his life to helping others less fortunate. He was quite pleased to hear God respond, "Yes, my son, you may win the lottery." The weekend passed and when he did not hit the jackpot, he figured God meant next week. The next week passed, then the third, and still he was not a winner. Very discouraged, he cried out to God, "Oh Gawd, why have you forsaken me? I thought you said I could win the lottery and then, as agreed, I would help others in need." God whispered, "Psst...hey, Boudreaux, first you have to buy a ticket."

In almost all cases that require action I think it is safe to say that any action is better than none. If high school graduates had to wait until they knew exactly what they wanted to study before they went to college, they would waste a lot of years trying to figure out what field interested them. Fortunately, by taking action and starting with basic introductory courses, students can discover what they don't like and eventually find their interests and talents. As life students, the same is true for us. Any action step moves you closer to your goal. It's the movement toward the goal that energizes the manifestation process.

My friend Sue learned that lesson after many painful years of being miserable in her job. Sue worked as a secretary at a local high school. She absolutely hated her job and loathed dealing with the mundane aspects of this particular position. When I asked her if she ever considered quitting, she said she couldn't because she needed the benefits. She kept waiting for the perfect job to appear like a knight in shining armor and whisk her away into career satisfaction. The perfect job never appeared. Out of desperation, she finally gathered up her courage and took action to change jobs. She worked with a florist doing delivery and small floral arrangements. It was far from the perfect job, but it was less tedious and she no longer felt tied down to her desk. As she learned more about plants she discovered that she much preferred being outside during the day. Sue soon came up with an idea for her own business. She started a small landscaping venture with a friend of hers. Together they grew plants and eventually developed a blooming business. Sue now says, "Had I not decided to move in just any direction, I would still be at Central High typing tardy reports for the principal's office and wishing I were dead. Today, I'm having the time of my life."

Talking about taking action is easier than doing it. All of us have areas in our lives that we are less inclined to take action in than others. There is a key word that will help you tremendously if you ever find yourself in need of taking action but feel stuck. This key word is *how* as in "*How* am I going to get what I want?" Creating an action attitude is achieved simply by eliminating any negatively framed *why* question and replacing it with a positively framed *how* question.

In my training to become a Gestalt therapist, I learned to avoid the word *why* in every therapeutic encounter with clients. "Why?" you ask. There are two reasons. First, the question *why* tends to activate the front or logical part of the brain. Because your brain is conditioned to come up with a reason, it will search its memory banks and, being clever and creative, it will give you an answer to the best of its ability. The catch is this: Because it is wired to always come up with an answer, it will find an answer—true or not—even if it has to make one up. Such answers often become incorporated into your basic belief system, thus leading to incorrect assumptions and unclear reasoning.

The second reason to avoid *why* is that the question itself presupposes that the question is based on fact. If I ask myself, "*Why* am I a failure?" my brain assumes that I am a failure, searches its memory banks for possible reasons, and comes up with the closest thing it can find. Possible answers to the question are "I wasn't my mother's favorite," "I'm too old," "I'm too young," "I'm not smart enough," or "I'm too much this or that." Once the *why* question is answered, you will notice that, as far as your brain is concerned, that's the end of the discussion, much like with parents who tell their children, "Because I said so, that's why." In other words, your brain gets the message: case closed, no room for discussion and, unfortunately, no need for action.

If, on the other hand, you were to inquire, "*How* can I be a success?" The brain says, "Hmm…success," and, presupposing that you must be capable of being a success, it searches for possibilities. It might come up with answers such as "I can read a book on success" or "I can study areas in my life in which I'm already using successful strategies and apply those to my new ventures." Perhaps it might say "I can study other successful people in this area and imitate their patterns for success."

How questions leave room for many answers and endless possibilities. You will continue to search for new possibilities until you are indeed the success you want to be. Changing *why* to *how* is very empowering and will help you to find opportunities where it seems none exist. Most important, *how* questions encourage action.

Another extremely important guideline to ensure clarity in action is to *always do what you say you will do.* Small commitments, when kept, become the foundation for power. Eventually small commitments build in size and scope. "I will save a dollar a day" grows into "I will retire in five years, living in my dream home." And a simple statement like "I will walk for ten minutes every other day" can one day become "I will run a marathon on my next birthday."

On those rare occasions when you do not keep your word, NO EXCUSES. Nothing is more diminishing to personal power than a lie or an excuse. Excuses erode your personal power by putting responsibility outside of yourself. If, for instance, I blame the traffic for my being late rather than taking responsibility and acknowledging that I didn't manage my time well, then I give traffic my power. The danger in doing this repeatedly is that I may eventually believe my excuses and feel as if I don't have any control over my circumstances.

Lies destroy personal power by splitting us and draining our energy. It takes energy to keep little white lies and stories straight. I like the saying "you are as sick as your secrets, and your sickness becomes your weakness." As a secret grows, your personal power diminishes.

This was demonstrated to me through working with Marlene, a psychotherapist in her midforties with whom I once worked. She sought my help when she discovered that she had a degenerative illness. When she had to take tests and treatments, she would do so in another town and tell her clients that she was on vacation. She occasionally went so far as to spend time in tanning salons to keep her clients' curiosity to a minimum. Her field was body/mind health and she was certain that if her clients knew her actual situation, they would see her as a phony or hypocrite and she would be out of business.

In the meantime she was losing all sense of joy, feeling weaker both physically and emotionally, and hating herself. When I suggested that she begin her healing journey by sharing her situation with just one client, she protested that she would probably lose her client by doing such a thing. I offered to pay for any lost income if that client left due to loss of respect for her. When I shared this offer with her she quickly refused and said, "You know, I really don't think that I'd lose my client. I think I am suffering from my own judgments." She realized she was probably harder on herself than anyone else would ever be. She agreed to tell at least one client and see how she felt.

When I saw her two weeks later, she looked like a new woman, at least ten years younger, no longer tired from hiding and travel. She had realized that if she wasn't hiding, she could take her treatments in town, which would save her a lot of energy. Not only did she tell her clients, but she told her colleagues and her friends as well. Before this time, only a few family members and her boyfriend knew her situation. She became excited and passionate about her work again, discovering and exploring even deeper levels of herself. As she began to live more powerfully by living in congruence with her truth, her clients sensed her authenticity and reported that they not only enjoyed working with her more but made faster progress as well.

Goals

The first three steps address clarity in desire. Steps 4 through 7 address clarity in action.

1. Write down in detail your life as you would like it to be on a daily basis for tomorrow, one year from now, five years from now, ten years from now.

2. Describe what you want to feel on your deathbed and make sure that your feelings are in alignment with your future goals.

3. Review your goals for tomorrow, one year, five years and ten years. Prioritize in order of importance.

4. Vividly visualize scenes in your life that allow you to experience already having achieved your goal. Remember to energize those scenes by making them seem real, in the present moment (as if they were happening in the here and now), and by using lots of emotion.

5. Break down your goals into the action steps you must take to reach your goals.

6. Take three action steps a day toward fulfillment of your goals. Remember, no excuses.

7. If you fail to keep a commitment, forgive yourself, select a simpler task and begin again.

Building power is a process. It happens in spurts, hits plateaus and sometimes includes periods of regression. It is very important to be kind to yourself during this particular exercise.

Clarity in Intuition

The fourth area to review for building and maintaining power is clarity in intuition.

What exactly intuition is, I cannot say for sure. Intuition, as I understand it, is knowing without knowing *how* you know. It is that little voice that we all hear from time to time when we are quiet or in need of guidance. Perhaps it is the voice of God. Whatever it is, it has helped to save my life on a few occasions. It has also helped me to counsel countless numbers of people in masterful ways that far exceeded my experience and ability.

One of my memorable encounters with my intuition happened to me on a pre-op hospital visit to evaluate Jamie, a ten-year-old girl who had eye cancer and required surgical removal of one of her eyes. She was scheduled for surgery the next day. Her parents and the staff were very concerned because no one had been able to get her to talk about how she felt about her surgery and the loss of her eye. I was a little apprehensive about our visit because I knew how important it was to get a baseline on her emotional state. Not only that, but I heard all of the horror stories of how she negatively reacted to all staff members including the nurses, psychologists, psychiatrist and social workers!

As I entered her room, she was seated on her mother's lap. She took one look at me and quickly wrapped her arms around her mother's neck. At that moment my intuition told me to ask her if she owned any stuffed animals. I recoiled at the thought of asking her that question because in my child development classes I had learned that was not an age-appropriate question and would alienate her. How "uncool" can you get—to ask a ten-year-old child if they own stuffed animals? (Even if they have them, at that age, it is considered a rather intimate piece of information.) I struggled quickly to think of a better question and told myself to ignore that little inner voice. After all, I didn't want to be embarrassed. But within seconds, I blurted the question out, "Jamie, do you have any stuffed animals?" She looked at her mother in an almost petrified way and shrieked "Mom, we forgot Bear! Oh no, we forgot Bear!" I found out later that she always brought her teddy bear to doctor visits and treatments.

By this time she was practically strangling her mother and the anxiety in the room had escalated a hundredfold. I was horrified. How dare my intuition do this to me. "This is the last time I trust that little voice!" I thought. And then, in another flash my intuition reminded me of a teddy bear in my office, which a patient had given me that day. In another flash I quickly excused myself and ran to my office down the hall. I picked up the huge teddy bear and ran back to Jamie's room, nearly out of breath and a little anxious that I might be digging a deeper hole to crawl out of. By now, I was committed to following through with my intuition and sure enough, what unfolded was nothing less than miraculous. As I entered her room, I asked Jamie if she would do me a big favor and "bear-sit" for me since I was going to be out of town for the next couple of days. She glanced at the bear, checked me out, then looked squarely into her mother's eyes and said, "Okay, Mom, you can leave now."

She then sat on the floor with me for two hours while we talked about boys and bears and eye surgery. We laughed and giggled and shared secrets with each other. By the end of the session, I had all of the information I needed to determine that she was well prepared for this surgery, and as I was leaving her room she gave me a friendship bracelet and a great big hug. That was just the beginning of a wonderful relationship for both of us. Though her little life ended all too soon, following my intuition created several opportunities for us that far exceeded anything I ever thought to be humanly possible.

For the record, I have to tell you that I am not always thrilled with what my intuition tells me. I don't like it when I become aware that a way I have been living or relating has become outdated for me. It means making a change that involves some degree of discomfort and effort. Nor is it always easy to share a new awareness with those I love, because many times they will be directly affected by it. One of the most difficult experiences I had with this was realizing that after more than thirteen years of being married to my wonderful husband, Greg, I no longer wanted to be in a married relationship with him. I had no logical and reasonable explanation. After all, our relationship was healthy, safe, loving and supportive. He was my best friend and someone who I not only trusted and loved dearly, but who I found to be a lot of fun as a life partner. However, over time I noticed an ever increasing restlessness and a knowing sense that I was no longer willing to be married to him. One afternoon, an image appeared in my imagination of a baby inside a womb. I asked my intuition what the meaning of this image was and immediately I knew that the "womb" was the safe and womb-like relationship I had with Greg and that the "baby" was me getting ready to move on after having been nourished by the relationship.

Though the experience was very painful, I managed to tell Greg that despite trying to will myself to be different, I could no longer deny the need to be divorced. His words to me immediately after my tearful announcement were, "Tina, do what you need to do. I trust you implicitly." Later, I thought, "How can I divorce someone who can be this supportive?" It was then that I realized it wasn't him who needed to trust me, but me who needed to trust myself and my intuition. Amazingly, the circumstances in my life, which seemed so difficult at the time, improved dramatically when I honored what was true for me. Although we shall always be "loves" for life, we have gone our separate ways and both have loving and fond memories of our separation and divorce. Although sad and grieving, we were both excited and hopeful about our separate new lives, and were already getting indications from our personal experiences that this decision was right for both of us. I can truly say that I have never felt more deeply peaceful, so profoundly passionate and so blessedly powerful in all of my life. I appreciate myself for doing my emotional homework, following my intuition and saying yes to what was true for me even though I didn't fully understand it.

Because taking action depends on deciding what course of action to follow, developing your intuition is critical when it comes to decision making. Most of us avoid taking action out of fear of making the wrong decision and therefore fear that we will take the wrong action. I doubt the existence of an absolutely right answer. I think the best we can hope for is to choose the best possible answer for ourselves, given our situation and our known resources at the time. If our situation or resources change, we can change our decision accordingly, but if most factors remain constant and we realize that the situation will not resolve itself, creating a reliable system of decision making is imperative. Without a reliable system, you can get bogged down in the process of thinking about thinking about your situation, or reacting to emotions alone, or taking action without giving thought to what is truly needed.

I would like to see an eleventh commandment that says "Thou shalt not postpone making a decision." This directive is important because procrastination is one of the easiest ways to lose energy and fail to take the action needed to fulfill your purpose. Leaving a decision unresolved for too long is very taxing to your mental, emotional and spiritual self and keeps you in a state of restless inertia. When you stand on one foot for a long period of time, you become unbalanced, and before you know it, begin to wobble and crash to the floor. In the same way, you can become mentally, emotionally, and spiritually unbalanced by leaving a decision up in the air for too long.

Making decisions with the head generally means the decisions will be logical, rational and even practical. The only area of decision-making where one can accurately rely on the head is in pure mathematics. To add two plus two and figure that they equal four requires only logic, but put a dollar sign in front of the numbers and have them represent your personal checking account and you will likely get an emotional response. Making decisions with the heart generally means the decisions will not be logical, rational or practical. But before you decide that heart-based decisions are worthless, it's important to remember that life itself is not a particularly logical or rational experience. Emotional feedback is necessary for proper decision-making ability. After all, if you have no positive or negative feelings about the consequences of a decision, then one decision is as good as another. Meanwhile, the nature of the gut is primal and borders on the mystical. Relying exclusively on any one system (head, heart or gut) results in an imbalanced way of living and gives precarious odds on making the decision that is right for you. Getting other points of view to give us a wider perspective certainly has value, but sometimes adding too many ingredients to the decision stew can create quite a mess. Rather than looking *outside* for more than one point of view, I think it is often better to find multiple points of view on the *inside*. This is where intuition and trusting inner knowledge are invaluable as life skills.

I believe the goal of therapy, or life coaching, is to assist you in becoming your own coach. When you rely too heavily on others such as parents, friends, therapists, psychics or teachers for advice, you weaken your ability to access your intuition. Over-reliance on others for coaching is like carrying a child until he is five or six years old. Normally, a child of that age would be quite capable of walking unassisted but, if he hasn't been allowed to walk, his muscles will have atrophied and he will be unable to move about on his own. In the same way, if you let others make or influence your decisions and do not exercise your own decision-making ability you will never develop confidence in your capability.

In my practice, I have seen many people experience great anguish and pain in the middle of trying to make a decision. I often hear "My heart says one thing, my head says another" or "I have a gut feeling this is the right thing to do, but every time I think about it, I change my mind." Trying to make a decision from two points of view is an unstable proposition that gives you only a fifty-fifty chance of making a decision that is right for you. An old family friend who once owned a dairy farm used to refer to anyone he didn't much care for as "about as useless as a two-legged milking stool." When a decision rests on balancing two points of view that are in conflict, you will feel as wobbly as a two-legged milking stool. Adding a third point gives you a three-centered decision-making system. The process is stabilized and less effort is required to maintain balance.

One method I have created to improve your access to intuition involves developing the three-centered decision-making system. This can be fun as well as extremely useful. It only requires a little imagination and a little practice to become proficient and feel more confident in your ability.

Three-centered decision making seems to work best if you get to know these three centers intimately: the head, the heart and the gut. The *head* is logical, practical, and rational. It frequently speaks in terms of *should*s and values. It has a *parental* quality. If you tend to be critical, refer to "The Language of Peace, Passion and Power" (chapter 1) and begin to reprogram your attitudes with nurturing words and tones. A nurturing parent is much more effective, not to mention more pleasant to deal with. The *heart* is emotional. It has a *childlike* quality; it is emphatic and more spontaneous in its response. The *gut* is primal and has a quiet power and a sense of knowing. It is very *adult* in its style.

Once you are familiar with the three different languages and styles of your centers, you are ready to begin to have an imaginary meeting, attended by all three centers, where they will agree to work together in your best interest in all future decisions. The head is the captain of the three-centered team, not because it is any more important than the others, but because of its verbal ability.

First, it is necessary to agree that majority rules. For example, if the head says no, but the heart and gut say yes, you have an affirmative decision. From then on, when you need to make a decision, invite all three centers to participate in a discussion of what is in your best interest from each perspective. Follow through with powerful action and notice how peace and passion reward you. Even choices that involve sadness and loss are followed by relief and freedom when you are listening to your three centers.

How you visualize the three centers is a matter of personal preference. Some people actually see organs at a round table. Others see the head personified as an intellectual character, the heart as an emotional character and the gut as a spiritually oriented person. Still others work on at auditory level, listening for words and tones. Start with small decisions until you feel comfortable with your ability to access your centers. Each center must be given the time and permission to express itself.

It is always comforting to arrive at a unanimous decision but many times two out of three must suffice. I have never received a negative report from anyone who has followed this procedure. Now and then a client has the experience of a split decision. One center says "yes," the other says "no" and the third says "I don't know." Split decisions mean the jury is still out and more reflection or information is needed before making a choice.

Once you can follow this procedure with ease, you may want to guess what your three centers will agree to do before you hold a decision-making meeting. This is an intuitive shortcut to the same process as described above.

Sally, a forty-two-year-old woman who has practiced three-centered decision making for several years, describes her imaginary team: "I see my head (the center of peace) as Sergeant Joe Friday from *Dragnet*. He is always calm, cool and collected and often says, 'Just the facts, ma'am.'

"My heart (the center of passion) is personified as a precious six-year-old girl. She is sweet and charming, very spontaneous and lots of fun, but yikes, when she wants something, she is demanding!

"I see my gut (the center of power) as an Asian woman, a Tai Chi master. She often speaks very softly and seems harmless enough, yet we all know how powerful she is. She is kind and often reminds my little girl self that she can have what she wants, but that *how* she gets what she wants is more important than responding impulsively. She teaches patience.

"I first used my 'team' when I was dating a man with a serious alcohol problem. My little-girl self (heart) adored him, he was so charming and lots of fun, when he wasn't loaded, that is. Sergeant Friday (head) laid out the facts. This man had a serious problem that required help. If he didn't seek professional help, the situation would only get worse. Ms. Tai Chi (power) was very calm and seemed sad as she reminded me that this relationship ultimately would become very destructive to all concerned. She comforted my child-self, who was by this time very upset. She assured my child-self that, if we refused to settle for less than what we are worth, we would eventually find a satisfying relationship.

"It was a very painful period for me. Every time I was tempted to call and work things out with this man, Sergeant Friday and Ms. Tai Chi would remind me of our agreement. The waves of temptation decreased in frequency and intensity. I woke up one morning and knew that I was healed and that I would never even be tempted to call him again. Three months later, I hit the jackpot. I met a man who was healthy and balanced. He was fun and playful but also serious and deep. He danced well, shared most of my interests and was financially well-established. His only addictions?

Jogging and world class lovemaking! One year later we were married, and we have so far lived happily and healthily together for five years.

"With their three seemingly unrelated characters, it is amazing to me to watch them work together to make decisions related to relationships, career and vacation time. I used to save them for really important decisions in my life, but the quality of their decisions was so impressive that I now often check in for little things. Last week I checked in for things like what to have for supper, what kind of exercise is best for me and so forth. I am amazed at how each part of me walks away satisfied and happy."

Clarity in Your Relationship
with a Power Higher Than Yourself

There have been occasions when I clearly envisioned my goal, set realistic action steps, lived honestly, listened to my intuition, and *still* hit a brick wall. It was during those times when I learned that even our most determined efforts can fail to bring us the goal we desire, and that perhaps at those times we are halted by divine intervention. For example, when I was inspired to create a retreat center in Louisiana, this inspiration became such a powerful dream that at times *it* seemed to dream *me*. I took action and was very successful, against many odds, at acquiring a beautiful piece of wooded property. Everything was sailing along smoothly and I began making plans for a magnificent multimillion-dollar facility. My plans swelled to include huge and complex buildings and a staff of at least twenty people. The original idea was to create a simple and peaceful environment for people to come to, to nourish body, mind and spirit.

But as the plans grew so did the challenges. It seemed like the project became a series of hardships, catastrophes and disappointments. Finally, the whole project came to a screeching halt. This was not just for a few days or weeks, but years. I was really angry with God and felt set up. After all, I had done my share of work on this project. In fact, I felt indignant, thinking I had done more than my share of the work. "Hey God, what ever happened to 'Ask and you shall be answered, seek and you shall find, knock and the door shall be opened to you'?" I grumbled. A friend of mine mentioned that I often bantered with God at times of stress when things weren't going the way I expected them to. She suggested I consider surrendering my will. "WHAT!!! You must be out of your mind," I thought. Just the word *surrender* gave me the creeps.

However, after a month of contemplation I had to admit that despite my Herculean efforts, there was a reason for the old saying "the best-laid plans of mice and men." Humbly, I came to the conclusion that we are not the ultimate creators of the universe. If we were, we would be able to create ourselves over and over again at will. Ultimate power for a human being is learning how to create with a force greater than ourselves. Call this power God, Goddess, All That Is, Spirit, the Universe, the Force, Mother Nature, Universal Energy Field, or whatever you find most comfortable. Rather than creating our reality, I believe we influence our reality on a daily basis. And the trick for me was to learn how to dance with this force gracefully. So I shifted from an attitude of "Hey God, this is what I want. Are you helping or not?!" to "This is what I feel is calling me, am I on track or not?" As I look back on my retreat project, I am thankful that I didn't have the resources at the time to create the well-intentioned but overdeveloped retreat center. I shudder as I see that I would have inadvertently created a Motel 6 with conference capability in the middle of the woods rather than a simple, quiet place to retreat. What I am creating now is much more the essence of my dream.

Even though most of my experiences with intuition have positive outcomes, trusting my intuition doesn't guarantee that everything will turn out exactly as I want it to. As I have learned to relax and trust my intuition, I have found that sometimes the results are less than what I hoped for. But many times, these days, the results far exceed my hopes and expectations. This is happening with more and more regularity. Manifesting has come to feel like a beautiful and exciting dance with God. Sometimes I take the lead and ask, "Oh God, wouldn't it be great if my life had this? And God responds, "Sure, and if you like, you can receive these little surprise blessings along the way."At other times God seems to be saying, "No, I don't think so."And though I don't understand at the time, I think, "Hmmm. There must be a reason; there must be something better for me in a different way." And sure enough, when I look back at my life, I see that not getting what I thought I wanted was a blessing, and, as a result, I got more of what I really needed.

I have also learned that when I begin to feel like I'm trying too hard, or that I'm pushing against the river, it may not be that my goal is off track, but that I am. Like the time I was bound and determined to have my entire house renovated by Christmas. A dear friend challenged my assessment of the situation and suggested I shoot for completing it by the Fourth of July. Insulted by his apparent lack of confidence in my ability to manifest, I blurted out, "I'll get this house finished by Christmas if it kills me!" He responded, "That's what I'm afraid of, Tina." He went on to remind me that I was exhausted and had been fighting a cold for three weeks. "Anybody can kill cancer if that's their goal," he said, "but the idea is not to kill the patient in the process." Taking his advice to heart, I kicked back a little and remembered to enjoy the process of renovating. I'm happy to report that not only did I enjoy the project but the house was finished by Valentine's Day. From that experience I learned that *how* something gets done is as important as (if not more important than) *that* something gets done.

Regardless of your beliefs about your source of power, I'm sure you'll find that the time it takes to develop your clarity in your life will be well worth it. And remember, you don't have to believe in water to get wet, but you do have to jump in. Start today, and take a few minutes every day to clarify and strengthen those five areas (mental and emotional life, desires, action, intuition, and your relationship to a power greater than yourself). Clarity is a safe, peaceful and passionate way to power. May the force be with you!

6
Training the Brain

It is impossible to begin a physical fitness program without preparing your body and equally impossible to begin an inner health program without preparing your mind. It is important to get your mind's attention and gently guide it to work to your advantage. I use various forms of meditation to get my mind's attention. Just as bathing is physical hygiene for the body, meditation is mental, emotional and spiritual hygiene for the mind and spirit.

Teaching your mind involves learning how to quiet your thoughts. A quiet mind is a powerful and flexible tool. With a quiet mind, you can program the body and mind to create what you wish to do, be or have. A quiet mind makes it easier to reprogram unfinished emotional business, heal childhood traumas, and locate sources of unconscious sabotage—all of which must be accomplished to create a greater sense of peace. A quiet mind also helps you in exploring new realms of emotional possibility. This is essential for creating passion. Finally, a quiet mind will help you to visualize your goals—a critical step towards mastering personal power.

Many people are unsure of themselves when beginning a mind training program. "I don't know how to visualize" and "I can't clear my mind" are two of the most frequent comments I hear. Because the meditative state is quite natural and easy to achieve and because it feels so comfortable, beginners who reach a meditative state are sure that it must be something else. "Why, this is just a relaxing of body and mind—like when I daydream!" one of my clients reported. Indeed, there is nothing strange or mysterious about the process at all. While many people still believe that hypnosis is a mysterious and unnatural state, it is in fact quite the opposite. The hypnotic state is a simple, healthy and very natural state of being that occurs when both the body and mind are relaxed. It occurs naturally at least twice a day whether you work at it or not, when you first wake up in the morning and just before you slip into sleep at night. It is characterized by being in an alert but not quite awake state. This state also happens spontaneously when you "space out" or daydream in the middle of the day. Unfortunately, most of us are taught to snap out of this state and get on with business. Too bad, because this quiet state of body and mind is a fertile environment in which you can practice visualization techniques to improve the quality of your life experience.

Visualization is a process of creating mental pictures for a specific purpose. There are as many purposes as you can imagine, for example, mental and physical healing, seeking inner guidance, creating and reaching goals or accessing your source of creativity. Some people use visualization simply for recreation and for the pure enjoyment of it. The most effective and powerful way to do visualization is while in a state of deep relaxation of body and mind, which can lead to rich states of altered consciousness.

Many are not aware of the value of these altered states of consciousness, and therefore pay little attention to daydreams or visual, mental images that occur between waking and sleeping cycles. Both daydreams and visual images arise from the unconscious and float quietly into our conscious awareness. There are many famous examples of brilliant inspirations that occurred during these states. One of the most well-known cases occurred when Friedrich Kekulé (1829–1896) awakened and recalled dreaming of a snake biting its tail. Upon contemplation, it occurred to him that bonded carbon atoms (which were thought to be stringlike structures) could actually be ringlike structures just like the image of the snake. The knowledge that carbons were capable of forming ringlike structures was the birth of modern organic chemistry, and a major contribution to a better understanding of the nature of life on a molecular level.

In daily practice, these states may give insight into your internal and personal world. I once worked with a man named Richard, who was in his early sixties. Richard was the picture of health. He was a marathon runner and an avid outdoor enthusiast. He came to see me because of a recurring dream in which he saw himself canoeing into a huge, heart-shaped canyon, where the water became muddy and the passage narrowed. The dream persisted, with the narrowing becoming smaller and the water getting muddier and thicker with each dream. In the last dream of its kind, the canoe guide turned to Richard and said, "If you don't get help, we are going to die soon." My interest was piqued when he described the heart-shaped canyon as "so much like a heart that sometimes the canyon walls seem to pulsate like a heartbeat." Despite his apparent excellent physical condition, I recommended a thorough physical exam, with a strong emphasis on his cardiovascular system to rule out any physical problems. Sure enough, he was diagnosed with a congenital defect in one of his coronary arteries, which was quickly narrowing to a dangerous degree and required immediate surgery. Had he not heeded his dreams, he was a likely candidate for a sudden and deadly heart attack.

Moments of relaxed body and mind can create images that are rich with inspiration. Sometimes we receive messages for healing or opportunities for greater self-awareness. Unfortunately, we have been conditioned to snap out of these moments and get back to business, thereby missing opportunities to be inspired or to give ourselves suggestions in the form of images that can enhance our lives. In addition to taking advantage of natural hypnotic states, we can create them at will by learning techniques to relax the body and mind. Remember, a hypnotic state is merely a deeply relaxed state of body and mind.

I am often asked if self-hypnosis is more effective than being guided into a hypnotic state by someone else. The answer is twofold. First, all hypnosis is self-hypnosis. Imagine your brain as a car with you as the driver. You are always at the steering wheel and always in control. A hypnotherapist would be a passenger who makes suggestions to you along the way. The therapist (passenger) might suggest, "Let's take a left turn here," but you are free at all times to take the left turn or not. Some people have negative images of hypnotism; they perceive it as a form of brainwashing that can force them to do something against their will. But brainwashing is a highly specialized and sophisticated process that involves the use of severe and extreme isolation and confusion techniques to break down a person's will. At some point in brainwashing, hypnotic techniques are used, but this process takes a great deal of time and occurs only under unusual circumstances that have no resemblance to current hypnotherapy.

Second, I suggest that you examine your preference for learning. Some people prefer to have a guide to instruct them, give feedback and answer any technical questions that may arise in the process. In this case, I wholeheartedly recommend having a guide to assist you in hypnosis. If you are looking for an easy way out, that is, if you want to have someone put you in a state of hypnosis, I am sure you can find a willing hypnotherapist somewhere. Although you might allow someone to guide you into a hypnotic state, hypnosis is a practice you can learn to do on your own. Most credible hypnotherapists will encourage you to learn how to use these techniques rather then telling you that hypnosis is something only they can do for you.

I encourage you to use hypnotherapists, audiotapes and other brain training accessories. Use them and learn from them until you are able to easily quiet and guide your mind. Some people go to a hypnotherapist to prove that they cannot be put in a state of hypnosis. Going in to prove that you can't be hypnotized can obviously limit the results you want. The best results are obtained if you go into a session with an open mind and positive intention.

Before hiring a trained hypnotherapist, review references to find one who is credible and understands the dynamic nature of this work. Hypnosis can cause the subject to feel somewhat open and vulnerable, so it helps to know that your guide is trustworthy and knowledgeable.

The more you understand how your brain works, the easier and more enjoyable you will find the process of hypnosis. Hypnosis (self-hypnosis or guided hypnosis) works because the brain does not understand the difference between what is real and what is vividly imagined. Thus you can convince your brain that your body and mind are capable of feats beyond your current experience. Hence the often-used phrase in the body-mind field, "What the mind can see and believe, it can achieve."

A Picture Is Worth a Thousand Practice Sessions

The power of the mind was clearly demonstrated in a study in which a basketball team was divided into three groups. The first group was asked to take three weeks off and neither think about basketball nor shoot baskets. The second group was asked to practice free throws for twenty minutes a day for three weeks. The third group was told to visualize themselves executing free throws for twenty minutes each day for three weeks, but not to physically practice at all. At the end of the study, the group that did no visualization or physical practice showed no improvement, as expected. The group that physically practiced free throw shooting had a 25 percent improvement. The group that only visualized had a 23 percent improvement. So there was only a 2 percent difference between those who physically threw the ball through the hoop and those who visualized it! Imagine what happens when you combine physical action with mental training! Could we double or triple our potential? No one knows for sure. We still cannot fathom the limits of our abilities with this powerful and synergistic combination.

Although we do not yet understand our limits and possibilities, we are learning more and more about how to enhance the effectiveness of visualization techniques. Research is now helping us to understand how and why emotions affect our ability to use the power of visualization to our advantage. The part of the brain associated with emotions, the limbic system, has some very interesting qualities and characteristics. For example, it does not understand time and makes no distinction between past, present and future. Everything is in the here and now. It is a very emotional system and doesn't understand words or logic. It is also a picture-oriented system, which means it thinks by seeing images and then responds with feeling. This is believed to be the part of the brain that gets emotional when experiencing powerful works of art. The saying "A picture is worth a thousand words" gets its meaning from the limbic system.

Much has been written about using affirmations (positive self-statements) in goal achievement. Affirmations are generated by the front brain (the cerebral cortex). Although they can be very effective, the pictures and symbols generated by the back brain (the limbic system) are even more so. Repeating affirmations over and over again eventually creates pictures that convince your mind that you can do or be whatever it is that you want to do or be. But wouldn't it be much more efficient to create a picture, drop it directly into the limbic system and allow it to be lived out through the body, mind and spirit?

The Power of Pictures

The power of imagery was demonstrated in a study of cardiac patients who experienced arrhythmia (an irregular heart rate). One group was asked to repeat affirming statements such as "My heart will beat at eighty-four beats a minute in a regular and rhythmic fashion." A second group was asked to visualize a child swinging rhythmically on a swing with her heart beating in time with the swing. The people in the latter group were able to slow their heart rates much faster than the control group members, who were asked to talk their hearts into beating at a regular rhythm and rate.

The more clearly you can create an image for the limbic system, the more emotion you will evoke and the more real the experience will become to the body-mind system. Goals that seem real (and therefore reachable) are accompanied by strong emotions, which stimulate another part of the brain known as the Reticular

Activating System (RAS). The RAS is designed to help us survive. If you were stranded in the desert without a source of water, the RAS would be activated by an urgent emotion: fear. Fear would alert your system that you were in need of water. Water would become top priority. Once this part of the brain is fired up, it goes into a "hunter" mode and creates a survival chant, which might sound something like "water, water, water, must have water." Once activated, the RAS discourages idleness: no stopping to gaze at birds flying overhead or daydreaming about the shapes of clouds. This part of the brain is all business and very focused, because it understands that the situation could mean life or death. Do or die. The RAS lets you know unequivocally that you must act.

When activated, the RAS transforms the brain into a survival mode. Awareness related to the achievement of the goal is heightened. Whereas merely gazing at birds overhead might be useless to the survival mind, studying the flight patterns of the birds for possible sources of water might be useful. And though daydreaming about clouds would be a waste of time, the survival brain turns something apparently wasteful into something useful, such as observing the clouds for potential rainfall and a source of water.

Most people in contemporary society have enough water to survive, food to spare, and shelter from weather and dangerous beasts, so the RAS doesn't have much of a job these days—unless we utilize its powerful potential to pursue our goals. Visualization allows us to create a clear, measurable goal with enough emotion to activate this system. The hunter goes into action and awareness is sharpened. When you know clearly what you want (your goal), your brain goes into hunting mode. You become sensitive to opportunities that may have been around you all the time, but which may not have been perceived as useful. And you can use those opportunities to fulfill your dreams.

Larry, a friend of mine, conditioned his RAS to become a hunter for financial freedom. He became a very successful millionaire by keeping his attention attuned to business opportunities to create the wealth he felt passionate about. His RAS was so conditioned to see financial opportunities that this way of seeing the world became second nature to him. One day, for instance, he was enjoying a good swim with a group of us in the Bahamas. When we got out of the water, a few members of the group began to complain about how sticky and stiff their hair felt because of the sea salt. He got quiet for a few moments and then brightened as he said, "Yes, that's it! The water could be used as a natural hair spray. We could call it Sea Spray. I wonder how cost-effective that would be." After a brief discussion we all determined that it wasn't a product any of us felt like developing.

Ten minutes later we were watching people enjoy banana boat rides. While we were laughing with the riders who fell off, Larry was calculating the cost per person and how many boats were active. He then began to determine whether it would be a viable business in Hawaii! He thoroughly enjoyed looking for business opportunities wherever his attention was focused, as his many business successes demonstrated. Larry learned to make a friend of his RAS and his RAS made a millionaire out of him. There is absolutely no reason in the world why you cannot do the same. Focus your mind on clear, multisensory, present-moment images, highlighted with strong emotions, and your dreams are on their way to you. You can take that to the bank!

The terminology of body-mind healing may seem intimidating or overwhelming to someone unfamiliar with the field. I have included a simple glossary for your convenience.

Terminology Associated with Brain Training

Meditation -Relaxing the body and clearing the mind of distracting thoughts in order to reach a state of deep relaxation of both body and mind, which produces a quietly wakeful and highly alert mental state

Transcendental Meditation (TM) -A highly popular form of meditation introduced to the United States in the 1960s, wherein an instructor gives the meditator a word or expression for a personalized mantra, which is repeated over and over during meditation to prevent distracting thoughts

Contemplation -Learning to look at an object, thought or situation in an alert and dynamic state that is free of ideation (mental thoughts)

Prayer -Verbal or mental communication with your spiritual source involving concentration (a mental focus) and a relaxed state of body and mind. The physiological response of the body to prayer is exactly the same as the response to a state of meditation

Hypnosis -An altered state of consciousness produced by a state of meditation supplemented with suggestions for changes in mental or physical behavior

Self-hypnosis -An altered state of consciousness produced when the practitioner enters a state of meditation supplemented by autosuggestion for changes in mental or physical behavior

Trance -A state of partly suspended animation or inability to function. A light trance is also known as a daydream. A deep state of hypnosis is characterized by a deep trance

Visualization -The process of creating a visual or mental image or picture for a specific purpose

Imagery -Mental images or products of the imagination

How to Visualize

There are several ways to create the quiet state of mind needed to practice visualization. The easiest is to deeply relax the body, which automatically helps the mind to relax as well. One technique for relaxing the body is deep breathing. To begin, take a deep breath, hold it briefly, and then exhale slowly and gently, allowing any tension in your body to release with the exhalation. After just two or three breaths you will find yourself in a much deeper state of relaxation.

Another way to relax is by practicing progressive muscle relaxation. To do this, you tighten or contract individual muscles of your body for several seconds and then relax them systematically, moving from head to toe. Imagery also can be a way to relax. To use imagery, create a mental image of a peaceful scene, imagine yourself in that scene and feel your body relax. At the end of this chapter I have included my personal favorite visualization exercise, which you may use as is or adjust to meet your own needs.

When I first began practicing visualization, I tried to imagine my son's face. Sometimes I could see his eyes clearly, but then I would notice that his ears weren't in the picture, or he was missing a chin, or the image was very fuzzy. I could only hold the image for a few seconds before it was gone, and then occasionally some bizarre image like the face of Yoda from *Star Wars* would appear and I was left discouraged. I thought maybe I was one of those people who just couldn't do it. However, I persisted, and with regular practice, I was soon able to create a full color, three-dimensional, panoramic view with stereophonic sound in my visualizations.

Visualization Continuum

To determine how skilled you are at visualization, do the following exercises:

1. Allow yourself to relax for a couple of minutes, clearing your mind as best you can from any distractions. Then imagine the face of someone you love and notice the details. Imagine him or her smiling at you and then walking toward you. Ask this person to tell you what he or she likes most about you and listen to the answer. Try to put yourself in this person's place so that you can see how he or she sees you. Imagine a fly on the wall and pretend that you become that fly and watch yourself and your loved one from the fly's eye view.

2. Return to a pleasant scene in the past that involved people. Notice the details. See how many of your senses you can involve in the scene. See if you can turn it into a still picture and then a moving picture. Try to make it slow motion. Bring your current self (dressed as you are) into the scene.

Pay attention to your feelings. See if you can interact with the people in the scene and somehow alter one or two aspects to make it more pleasant (such as the light, sound, what someone says or does for you).

3.   Imagine a tall, clear crystal vase filled with daisies. Change the color of the vase to blue, then red, then green, then back to clear; then watch the daisies turn pink, and then become pink roses. Imagine taking the pink vase with pink roses to someone you love next week, and see his or her expression as you present your gift.

Review the technical quality of your visualization by comparing it to the table of attributes below.

A

- Fuzzy images or impressions
- Flat, two-dimensional pictures that look like photographs
- Partial picture that fades or disappears
- Black and white image
- Only one sense is involved in image
- Still picture
- Only able to see image from one point of view (either associated or dissociated)
- Unable to change or "morph" image
- Dialogue and action seem forced and contrived
- Only able to see in one time dimension

Total:

B

- Clear images, not much detail
- Image looks more real than a photograph but lacks depth
- Almost complete image that can be sustained for thirty seconds or two minutes

- Basically black and white with occasional bits of color; or an all-color image, but with muted dull tones
- Visual imagery is accompanied by at least one other sense (sound, taste, smell, touch)
- Choppy or awkward motion
- Able to see image from associated and dissociated points of view
- Able to change image in one or two ways (size, shape, color, speed, volume, etc.)
- Dialogue and action have moments of spontaneity but still require some prompting
- Able to recall past events and imagine present-moment images

        Total:

C

- Clear, crisp images with plenty of detail
- Image has depth and three dimensions
- Total picture lasts indefinitely
- Technicolor (even some advanced practitioners do not see in color)
- Many or all senses are included
- Smoothly moving pictures
- Able to see image from multiple points of view
- Complete and quick morphing ability
- Dialogue and action become spontaneous and seem to take on a life of their own
- Recall past, imagine present, and create alternative pasts and futures

        Total:

Scoring:
- A—You are a visualization weakling. Don't be discouraged, you have plenty of room for progress.
- B—You are an intermediate visualizer. You can do powerful work already.
- C—You are an advanced visualizer. Your dreams are on their way.

Practice visualization for ten to twenty minutes a day for three weeks, then repeat the above exercise. You may be surprised at how much you see the second time.

Brain Training Tips

During many years of practice and study, I have collected information on brain training. The following information has been valuable to me; you may find these tips useful.

1. The brain does not know the difference between what is real and what is vividly imagined. Visualization of your goal is most effective when it seems as real as possible and is perceived as if it is occurring in the present moment or has already happened.

2. The recommended time of day to meditate is usually in the quiet of early morning. The recommended length of time is twenty minutes. The recommended position is a comfortable seated position. Lying down is not advised because most of us fall asleep! Listen to your body and mind to determine what works best for you.

3. Regularity and consistency are the keys to a successful meditation practice; therefore, feel free to adjust times of day, lengths of sessions, and positions to meet your specific needs. Lawrence LeShan, author of *How to Meditate*, reminds us, "Do not expect to do a meditation 'well' (focusing on it and nothing else) for a long period of time. The important thing about meditation is how hard and consistently you work on it, not how well you do it. This point cannot be overstated. It is a crucial truth, but most

people simply do not believe it."

4. The more senses it involves, the more effective a visualization exercise will be. If you not only picture a scene, but actually hear and feel and perhaps even taste and smell the different aspects in the picture, it will seem more vivid, more real to the brain and, therefore, more powerful.

5. Energizing the scene with emotion can also enhance effectiveness. In other words, seeing your savings account with a large balance won't propel you into action nearly as quickly as if you imagine how secure and happy you will feel while enjoying your wealth.

6. Seeing a scene as if you are actually experiencing the situation firsthand is much more intense than observing yourself in the scene as if you were watching yourself in a movie.

7. Practice makes possible. The more you practice, the more easily you will achieve that which you visualize.

8. Your mind is like a muscle. Your ability to concentrate and remain focused will increase with time and practice.

9. Once you perfect the technique, even though you may stray from practicing meditation or visualization for long periods of time, you will find that it doesn't take long to return to a high level of functioning.

10. Even if your image is fuzzy, incomplete, or can only be sustained for a few seconds, a little practice will move you quickly to a higher level of imagery. As you practice, your ability to sustain images will improve as will the clarity and creative quality of your visualizations.

11. You are probably already better at visualizing than you think. Most people don't realize that they visualize every day. Think of someone you love, close your eyes and try to see them smiling. If you can, then you are already able to consciously create a visual picture.

12. Most practitioners notice benefit from this practice in approximately three weeks, although some people report benefits immediately and others take longer. Reported

benefits include more energy and more creativity; and feeling healthier, more relaxed and less upset by the stresses of life.

13. With even more practice, you will eventually hit what I call the "sweet spot" in which you will be able to observe your thoughts and emotions without judgment. Hitting the sweet spot creates greater clarity and freedom internally as you see the truth of who you are and who you are not. This particular stage of development is the most difficult to explain. It is like the difference between reading about oranges and tasting one.

My All-Time Favorite Visualization

Get into a comfortable position. You may want to close your eyes to relax more deeply. Become aware of your breathing. Slow your breathing. Take a deep breath, hold it and become aware of the tension you feel across your chest and throughout your body. Exhale gently as you silently say the word "relax." Feel your muscles letting go and become aware of the tension leaving your body. Again, take a deep breath and hold it. Feel the tension across your chest, back and entire body. Once again, as you exhale, gently and silently say the word "relax" to yourself. If you notice any noise in your environment, let it be merely a reminder to you to let go and relax more deeply.

In your imagination, begin to see yourself walking along your private beach. See the ocean waves and hear the gentle song of the ocean. The waves rock you rhythmically to the sound of your breath, in and out, in and out. See the sky, the clouds, and the sun. Hear the birds in the distance. Find a spot that is safe and secluded, and as you lay down by yourself to rest more deeply, imagine yourself as a pat of butter on the sand. Allow the warmth of the sun to massage your muscles, and feel any last bit of tension melt away.

From this relaxed state, gently rise to take a walk along your private beach. Feel the sand beneath your feet and the warmth of the sun on your shoulders. You can almost smell and taste the ocean salt in the air. Look out into the water; two dolphins are waiting for you. Wade into the water and grasp each dolphin by the dorsal fin, allowing them to bring you gently out into the water. Notice that you feel no fear. Intuitively, you know that when you begin to go into the water, you will be able to breathe as easily and freely as if it were air. As you become aware, go deeper into the water, and with each exhalation feel yourself relaxing, letting go and feeling more and more peaceful. Each exhalation brings you deeper and deeper into the depths of the ocean, letting go and relaxing more and more deeply. When you reach the ocean floor, notice the soft light and how everything on the ocean floor moves very slowly as if you are in a bowl of comforting, soothing, gently moving Jell-O being swayed slowly, slowly, slowly to one side and then slowly and gently back. It is very, very quiet; so quiet that you can hear your thoughts. Ask yourself what you hope to obtain in this quiet state of deep relaxation. Then:

- If you are seeking guidance, look for a huge seashell that begins to open as you approach. Inside the shell is a guide who will give you instructions, a symbol, information or an inspiration to help you with a particular challenge that you are facing.
- If you are seeking deeper relaxation, feel the ocean rocking you gently into a more and more deeply relaxed state of being.
- If you are seeking healing, ask one of the sea creatures to take you into the deep chambers of the ocean floor so that you can have an experience of emotional or physical healing.
- If you are interested in goal achievement, see yourself in the situation you want to create. Feel yourself being, doing or having whatever you desire. Experience it as if it is happening now in the present moment.
- If you seek recreation or creative inspiration, or if you are interested in exploring your unconscious, then continue to relax and allow the visualization to unfold, creating an experience to inspire or entertain you.

When you have gained a sense of whatever you are seeking, call the dolphins back. With a hand on each dorsal fin, allow them to bring you back to shore, while becoming more and more aware with each inhalation. As you inhale, feel yourself become lighter, energized, refreshed, vital and ready for a new day. Feel your back, your body, and then gently stretch as you become aware of your surroundings, feeling refreshed and awake as if you have had a very peaceful and refreshing deep sleep.

No-Thought or Quiet-Mind Meditation

A quiet mind is a powerful and flexible mind. Visualization is a potent device that enables us to tap into our human potential and create endless possibilities. The other form of brain training, which I call *no-thought* meditation, helps us to embrace our humanness without judgment. This is a point of entry into spiritual growth and awareness.

Once comfortable with the practice of visualization, I began to include no-thought meditation in my sessions. I was immediately distressed at how my mind would flit all over the place like an uncontrollable butterfly. My internal conversation sounded something like, "Okay, I think I am getting this because I am not thinking...Wait a minute, if I'm not thinking, what am I doing right now? Aw, I guess I'm thinking! Okay, let's see, let's get back to not thinking...Uh-oh, I forgot to write down 'pick up clothes at dry cleaners.' I wonder if I'll have time to stop at the coffee shop and pick up a little something for Sue's birthday tomorrow. Is this her thirty-eighth or thirty-ninth birthday?...Hey wait, whoa, quiet...quiet...okay...good...(*Silence*)...Oh, yes! I'm not thinking!...Wait a minute, oh darn, I'm thinking again. Oh well, I wonder what we'll have for lunch today?..." One of my yoga teachers describes the moment one becomes aware of proficiency in meditation as the Law of the Good Moment, or "Here I am, wasn't I?"

Years later, I am still not perfect at no-thought meditation. I understand that no one is, but I now realize it is the effort of the exercise that brings the benefit to the practitioner. As with everything, you will get better with consistent effort. It has become such a habit for me that I usually don't leave the house without having some quiet time.

If you are ready to attempt no-thought meditation, which is the purest and perhaps most difficult form of meditation, you must begin by quieting your mind. This is commonly accomplished by concentrating on the breath. Sit or lie in a comfortable position. Allow your thoughts to become very quiet. Empty your mind of all thought. When you become aware of a thought, simply observe it and return your attention to breathing. Simple as it sounds, it requires the most discipline of all meditation techniques, but it will quickly condition you to a higher level of mental strength. Just as practicing visualization helps prepare the brain for no-thought meditation, no-thought meditation also enhances the process of visualization.

Because of the inherent difficulty in no-thought meditation, I believe it also requires the most self-compassion. As we see how much stuff we think about and how our minds chatter endlessly, we may be tempted to be self-critical and become frustrated. To develop compassion within yourself, remember: Frustration means you are expecting more from yourself than you are capable of delivering at that moment. Back up and accept that you are doing the best you can, given your history, chemistry and present-day situation. This is the kind of understanding angels are made of!

No-Thought Breathing Techniques

Here are three suggested methods of concentrating on your breathing in order to quiet your mind:
1. Quietly inhale through your nose to the count of four. Hold your breath and count to eight. Gently exhale through your mouth to the count of four. Repeat for approximately ten cycles and thereafter whenever your awareness strays.
2. Imagine that the ambient air is breathing you (instead of vice versa). Then bring your attention to the air that passes

through your nostrils at the tip of your nose. Simply say to yourself "in breath" with each inhalation and "out breath" with each exhalation. After a few minutes allow your mind to coast into a no-thought state. If thoughts appear and do not immediately disappear, return to "in breath" and "out breath" breathing.

3   Inhale and say "One," hold the breath briefly while saying the word "and," then say "one" with the first exhale. Repeat the second round: "Two" (inhaling), "and" (pause briefly holding the breath), "two" (exhaling). The third round is "Three" (inhaling), "and" (pause briefly holding the breath), "three" (exhaling). If you find your attention straying from the breathing and counting, immediately return to "One, and, one." Continue in this manner until you reach "Ten, and, ten," at which point you can begin no-thought meditation. If you begin to think, it's back to "One, and, one."

7

Permission to be Less Than Perfect

The most elegant way I know to move toward transcending our humanness is to *embrace* our humanness, accept our imperfections and be kind and gentle with ourselves. If we do so, all of the concepts presented in this book become welcome friends who show the way to personal freedom and liberation from unnecessary pain. They guide us to peace, passion and power. When my son Matthew was sixteen years old, he announced that if support groups for ACOA (Adult Children of Alcoholics) were so helpful for so many people, there was a need for a new support group called ACOT to help adult children of therapists. He then gave the following monologue: "When I was growing up, I always felt like the odd kid out. While the other kids were name-calling and teasing, I was thinking, 'They're doing the best they can.' I could never feel 'just okay' with a therapist mother. I had to describe my feelings: I feel hurt, mildly annoyed or really angry. Of course, I had to be careful with the words I used because my subconscious was always listening. In our home, problems were called 'challenges' and there was no such thing as 'failure,'" only 'feedback.'"

We all got a good laugh out of Matthew's announcement and still joke about the "challenges" of growing up in a minimally dysfunctional family. But his words echoed in my ears: "There was no such thing as failure, only feedback." I don't remember ever saying those words, yet as I reviewed our lives, I realized that "feedback rather than failure" was an ingrained attitude of mine that he had internalized.

I remember well when he was twelve years old and I asked him to take roller skating classes with me. I later overheard him telling a friend, "Yeah, well, you know how when your grandmother wants to go play bingo, and you go to be a nice guy? Well, my mom wants to learn how to skate, so I'm going to take skating classes with her." In that spirit, we began skating classes. There I was, protected with knee and elbow pads. If I had owned one, I would have worn a helmet! I was very careful, skating forward gingerly, and even more tentatively backward. Matthew skated with total abandon. While he was learning, he fell more times than I could count. He slammed into walls, got rolled over once or twice, and basically looked quite awkward most of the time. It never occurred to him that other people might be laughing at him or making fun of his lack of gracefulness. When the six-week course was over, I was just learning to skate forward smoothly and skating backward only slightly better than when I started. Meanwhile, Matthew was doing incredible one-leg backward dips, flips, swirls and jumps like someone who had been skating since he could walk! He had learned from his mistakes and taken lots of chances; therefore, his proficiency at skating was much greater than mine.

Six years later, Matthew joined the Air National Guard. He called home from training camp, chuckling that he had been assigned to a welding class and was absolutely the worst welder in the group. In eight weeks, after discovering all of the ways not to weld, he eventually became a very skilled welder. In fact, he became the best welder in the class and graduated with honors.

As Matt demonstrated, we learn better and perform better when we are free to explore all options in the process. Exploring all the options generally involves making a few mistakes. And mistakes, unfortunately, are often regarded as failures. The threat of failure seems to evoke fear in many of us, robbing us of our ability to flow freely and enjoy passionately whatever we may be involved in at the time. I think it is much like asking someone to walk across a balance beam. If it's on the ground, we can walk, run or even dance across it. But if that same two-by-four is ten feet in the air, most people become more tentative because the stakes are higher. One way we mentally raise the stakes and scare ourselves is by losing perspective and telling ourselves that if we fail we'll be embarrassed and humiliated. I think the secret to reaching our potential and enjoying it passionately lies in lowering the stakes.

We sometimes wrongly perceive the stakes as high due to our sense of fear or apprehension of approaching anything new. In other words, we assume that because we are nervous and scared, something must be wrong. But for the sake of survival, human beings are wired to be cautious about new situations. Please note that caution does not mean "wrong" or "stop," it simply means "be careful."

Fulfilling our potential requires that we release our fear-based misperceptions. One of the most crippling of these is perfectionism—which is a fear of failure. If we choose to see the outcome of our actions as feedback rather than failure, we remove the specter of urgent, frightening, incapacitating, immobilizing and paralyzing consequences. Instead, we can see the outcome as simply a learning experience, and feedback along the way as information that lets us know there is more to be learned to reach our goal.

I wish I had been following my own advice about three weeks ago when I created my self-imposed deadline to complete this book. I had a rather difficult day. Nothing extraordinarily awful happened, but it was a very long day filled with minor disappointments. I had planned my evening to be free to write and edit, but found myself too tired to be creative. I felt frustrated and disappointed. Before I knew it, I had slipped into a full-blown funk. I even threatened to set my manuscript on fire, saying, "I don't feel peaceful, passionate or powerful! In fact, I feel like an emotional, whining wimp!" I checked my calendar. No, it wasn't PMS! I had been eating fairly well all day long and could detect no hypoglycemia. I was just in a funk.

Then I thought about all of the dynamic, powerful, inspirational leaders and teachers I know who practice what they preach. I thought about my life and my practice and knew that I, too, practice what I preach. I preach imperfection and I practice it perfectly! If I can live in harmony and balance with ever-growing amounts of peace, passion and power at least eighty percent of the time, then I am also doing phenomenally well. Living peacefully, for me, involves embracing my humanness—which is imperfection personified—and accepting that I am doing the best I can, given the circumstances. So that night I popped some popcorn, had a beer and watched a mindless video. It was a wonderful night.

One side effect of the human potential movement is the extreme emphasis on positive thinking and seeing people as self-help projects rather than works of art in progress. From a self-help project point of view, there is always something wrong that needs to be fixed or at least improved. Personal growth becomes a monumental task requiring serious study and enormous amounts of self-discipline. When growth is seen as a job or a series of tasks and accomplishments it loses its elasticity and is robbed of the passion that is inherent when growth is seen as an exploration and creation of a work of art in progress.

Extreme task thinking can have a rebound effect, such as when we get down on ourselves for not being "positive" enough or for simply being human. Always feeling compelled to be super positive and improve ourselves can result in a counter-productive, passion-sapping state and lead to a personality without dimension. Sometimes life stinks! Sometimes life is just not fair! And sometimes I want to feel sorry for myself. So be it.

As human beings, we can only drive ourselves until we reach an invisible ceiling which stops us from growing further in what we want to accomplish in life. You can only *drive* yourself so hard for so long before you deplete your resources. However, when you are *drawn* to that which inspires you, you tap into an unlimited well of energy.

I figure that if computers have down time, human beings can

too. And I reserve my right to be perfectly human! (Now there is an oxymoron for you—"perfectly human.") I encourage you to give yourself the option of experiencing down time when you are not feeling strong or healthy or in balance. Do it without judgment. I believe that down time at its best may be a sort of creative stew out of which comes clarity and creativity. Sara Ban Breathnach, author of *Simple Abundance*, refers to this down time as "sacred idleness." I love that term because it respects the nurture of the soul that comes from steeping in this space.

Anyone who has ever cleaned out a closet has experienced the chaos that precedes the neatly organized completion of the task. Pulling things out of the closet and looking at the jumbled mess beneath our feet, we begin to ask necessary questions. "Do I still want this or that?" "Am I ready to let this go?" In the same way, down time allows us a chance to look through our mental, emotional and spiritual closets to determine what is working and what is not, and then consider implementing changes to help us stay alive and vital. It cuts out the dead and useless baggage we carry so we can be energized for what we want to create.

The thought of down time can be rather uncomfortable if you always demand perfection of yourself. If down time is a difficult concept to embrace, hold on, because I am going to suggest that you not only give yourself permission to slow down and be idle, but that you also give yourself permission to stop. As a recovering perfectionist myself, I certainly feel qualified to say, "Attempting to be perfect in an imperfect world is not only futile, but it can be destructive to body, mind and soul."

If down time or "time-out" seems too hard to imagine at this stage in your life, you may want to consider giving yourself permission to be imperfect. If I managed to accomplish such a feat, surely you can too. My breakthrough with permission to be human (to be imperfect) started years ago when my dad and I were digging a garden. I asked him if he thought we should dig a little deeper. He said, "You know what I always say, 'If you are going to take the time to do something, do it right.' I looked at my mother and said, "So that's where I got my perfection tape!" She smiled and said, "I

heard him say, 'Do it right,' but I didn't hear the word 'perfect'."
There I was, a thirty-something adult with a HUGE imprint to be
perfect. But for the first time in my life, I was able to hear that there
is a difference between doing something right (which I now think
means "good enough") and doing something perfectly (which I
now thinks means "neurotic"). That's when I realized that as
children we sometimes distort messages, which remain larger than
life in our imprinted memory.

For example, as a young adult I was shocked when I returned
to the grammar school I had attended as a youngster and saw how
tiny the playground had become! I would have bet a hundred
dollars that it was at least twice as big as it was, but I didn't take
into account that back then I was half the size I am today. I
wondered if other messages I received as a child were equally out
of proportion. I realized at that moment that I was in desperate need
of permission to make mistakes and to release myself from a
limiting imprint (perfectionism) that kept me from peace.
Furthermore, I realized that I had to make this change regardless of
whether it was an actual or perceived message that I had imprinted.

Shortly after this realization, I did a visualization exercise in
which I gave myself permission to be human and imperfect. My
childlike self had some difficulty with this, fearing she would be
abandoned if she made mistakes, but I assured her that everything
would be better and it would be a much easier way to live. Little did
I know at the time that within the week, I would make a mistake
that would sorely test my new resolve. I was at a Mardi Gras parade
and had a little more alcohol than was my custom and I shocked
myself by passionately kissing a friend of a friend, whom I had
never met before! I felt totally embarrassed and humiliated. I
repeatedly apologized to my husband, saying, "Greg, I can't believe
I did that!" Finally, Greg said, "Tina, please don't worry. Hey, it's
Mardi Gras! Besides, I think you've had a little too much to drink."
I responded, "Yes, but I knew what I was doing!"

For the next twenty-four hours, I continued to obsess about
the situation. I shredded myself for my inappropriate behavior.
Then, in a flash, I realized that what I had done was not perfect, and

that if given the situation again, I would do it differently. I accepted the fact that I had made a mistake by overstepping my own boundaries of acceptable behavior and forgave myself for being human, imperfect and drunk. Instantly, all feelings of embarrassment and shame vanished!

Later, I had a chance on the job to try out my new-found peace. I was called to the hospital director's office. As I heard the tone of her voice calling for me over the intercom, I got that sinking feeling, reminiscent of being summoned to the principal's office. Sure enough, I had made a serious mistake by assigning a client to a therapist who was not certified by the client's insurance company. Unfortunately, the therapist and client had already developed rapport, and separating them would have been traumatic to the client. I found myself looking at my signature and saying very maturely to the director, "Yes, this is my handwriting. I don't know what I was thinking when I did this. I can assure you I understand the seriousness of this mistake. I will see that, to the best of my ability, it does not happen again." I felt very adult, mature, responsible and very powerful. I was proud of myself for not making excuses or denying what was obviously my mistake, and on the inside, I was dancing! I was rocking and rolling, just imagining myself saying to the director, "So what are you going to do, *hang* me?!? I am HUMAN!" It was quite a liberating experience for me. (Let me note that the importance of being more mindful at work did not escape me. I was much more careful after that incident and did not repeat that particular mistake.)

From then on, my internal response to mistakes has continued to be rather neutral, with an occasional sense of relief and pride in the fact that I no longer put myself through the "How could I have done that?" interrogation. Mistakes no longer have a paralyzing effect on me. And since making mistakes no longer carries that stinging, whiplash effect, I find that I can more easily try things and enjoy them more peacefully, passionately and powerfully. Because, after all, what's the worst thing that can happen to me?

Shortly after that experience, I began to share my imperfections with my clients, a few of whom were therapists themselves. At first I felt a little reluctant, fearing that they might lose respect for me, and that I might lose business if I disclosed my own struggles. Sometimes I would say, "I am not sure if I can help you with that particular issue, because I am dealing with the same thing right now. But if you're willing, we can explore it together. Maybe we can leapfrog on each other's experience." Instead of reacting negatively to my situation, my clients felt relieved to discover that there was a lot of room for being human in our world, both for them and for me. We came to the conclusion that no matter how healthy and balanced we are, all of us have pockets of craziness. I have experienced more peace at work since then and no longer feel pressured to be the perfect therapist and always have the right answers. My clients' respect for me has increased tremendously, and their growth has accelerated considerably. Best of all, I enjoy my work more passionately than ever.

Seven Steps to Busting Perfectionistic Thinking

Observe any talents and skills you have that don't flow when others are present because you fear failure. Lower the stakes by asking yourself, "What is the worst thing that can happen if I don't accomplish my goal?" and "How can I turn this into feedback?" Make a conscious decision to remove the word "failure" from your vocabulary.

Practice any action you think to be foolish and silly in public. Notice how easy it is to survive the experience. It may feel a little awkward at first, but you will find that you feel less discomfort as you become more and more playful and spontaneous. Write down ten silly things you can do this week and do them. Come on now— I made a space for this just for you:

Ten Silly Things to Do to Stretch Yourself into a More
Spontaneous You

1._____

2._____

3._____

4._____

5._____

6._____

7._____

8._____

9._____

10._____

Read Susan Jeffers's book, *Feel the Fear and Do It Anyway*.

Notice how you can relate to and be inspired by the imperfection and authenticity of others. Joseph Campbell, author of *Hero's Journey*, believed that human beings have difficulty relating to perfection, which is why he believed that people could relate to Jesus Christ and his humanness more easily than to an all-perfect, all-knowing God. If you find that perfectionism is an issue for you, do an inner child visualization in which you give yourself permission to be less than perfect. Remember, it doesn't have to be a perfect exercise. Good enough will do!

Forgive yourself for being human next time you make a mistake. Remind yourself that you are doing the best you can. Congratulate yourself when you are able to forgive yourself. As you get more experience, you will notice that the time between your mistake and the ensuing self-forgiveness will decrease. Journaling about this will help you track your progress.

Hint: Be gentle with yourself. A few backslides along the way are part of the process.

Give yourself some optional thoughts and behaviors for future conditioning. Look for safe and appropriate opportunities to share your mistakes and imperfections. You will notice that this type of sharing decreases your overall tension and releases you from the burden of trying to act perfect. Sharing imperfection fuels your passion associated with enjoying who you are, mistakes and all. It also affords others the opportunity to share their humanness and feel more intimately connected with you.

Schedule some preventive down time to give yourself a chance to revive, and mentally, emotionally and spiritually putter about. Thirty minutes of down time could spare you a week of recovery from burnout.

If you want a surefire way to screw up your life, try this method: Use this book (or any other self-help book, for that matter) and work very hard to be perfect. You will become unhealthy faster than you can say "Uh-oh." I used to think there was a perfect balance point in my life and that once I hit that point, I could just stay there and my life would be in balance forever. What I didn't realize at the time was that the balance point is constantly changing. Rest and relaxation become boring once I am restored. Exciting and growth-stimulating situations can eventually become frenetic and chaotic if experienced for too long.

So, in the spirit of love, and embracing your human-ness, I hope as you look back on your life in your last moments before death, you will feel the peace and satisfaction that comes from having had a life well-lived. I hope you will be able to see that what you accomplished was on purpose most of the time and that you used your power wisely to improve the quality of your life and the lives of those who were blessed to be touched by you.

Embrace and enjoy, for our time on Earth is brief.

Bibliography

Andreas, Steve. *Change Your Mind and Keep the Change.* Moab, Utah: Real People Press, 1990.

Baldwin, Christina. *Life's Companion: Journal Writing as a Spiritual Quest.* New York: Bantam Books, 1991.

Bandler, Richard, and John Grinder. *Frogs into Princes: NeuroLinguistic Programming.* Moab, Utah: Real People Press, 1979.

Benson, Herbert, MD. *The Relaxation Response.* New York: Avon Books, 1975.

———. *Beyond the Relaxation Response.* New York: Berkeley Publishing Group, 1985.

Bolen, Jean Shinoda, MD. *The Tao of Psychology: Synchronicity and the Self.* San Francisco: Harper & Row, 1979.

Boudreaux, Curt. *The ABC's of Self-Esteem.* Abita Springs, Louisiana: Synergy Press, 1996.

Bradshaw, John. *Homecoming.* New York: Bantam Doubleday Dell, 1992.

Center for the Practice of Zen Buddhist Meditation. *That Which You Are Seeking Is Causing You to Seek.* Mountain View, California: Keep It Simple Books, 1990.

Chopra, Deepak, MD. *Quantum Healing: Exploring the Frontiers of Mind/Body Healing.* New York: Bantam Books, 1989.

Coelho, Paulo. *The Alchemist: A Fable about Following Your Dream.* New York: Harper San Francisco, 1993.

Cousins, Norman. *Anatomy of an Illness as Perceived by the Patient.* New York: Bantam Books, 1991.

Davis, Martha, Elizabeth Robbins Eshelman, and Matthew McKay. *The Relaxation and Stress Reduction Workbook.* Oakland, California: New Harbinger Publications, 1995.

DeLaney, Gayle. *Living Your Dreams*. San Francisco: Harper Publications, 1996.

Dychtwald, Ken. *Body-Mind*. New York: St. Martin's Press, 1986.

Dyer, Wayne W. *Your Erroneous Zones*. New York: Avon Books, 1976.

————. *You'll See It When You Believe It*. New York: Avon Books,1990.

Feinstein, David, and Stanley Krippner. *Personal Mythology: Using Ritual, Dreams, and Imagination to Discover Your Inner Story*. New York: St. Martin's Press, 1988.

Fields, Rick. *Chop Wood Carry Water: A Guide to Finding Spiritual Fulfillment in Everyday Life*. New York: G.P. Putnam's Sons, 1984.

Gawain, Shakti. *Creative Visualization*. New York: Bantam New Age Books, 1978.

————. *Living in the Light*. New York: Bantam New Age Books, 1993.

Goleman, Daniel. *Emotional Intelligence*. New York: Bantam Books, 1995.

Goleman, Daniel, and Joel Gurin. *Mind Body Medicine: How to Use Your Mind for Better Health*. Yonkers, New York: Consumer Reports Books, 1993.

Hendrix, Harville. *Getting the Love You Want*. New York: Harper Collins, 1989.

Hittleman, Richard. *Guide to Yoga Meditation*. New York: Bantam Books, 1969.

Jampolsky, Gerald G., MD. *Love is Letting Go of Fear*. Berkeley, California: Ten Speed Press, 1979.

Jampolsky, Gerald G., MD., and Diane V. Cirincione. *Love Is The Answer: Creating Positive Relationships*. New York: Bantam Books, 1990.

Kübler-Ross, Elisabeth. *Living with Death and Dying*. Tappan, New Jersey: McMillan Publishing, 1982.

LeShan, Lawrence. *How to Meditate*. New York: Bantam Books, 1974.

McMahon, Susanna. *The Portable Therapist*. New York: Dell Publishing, 1992.

Ornish, Dean. *Dr. Dean Ornish's Program for Reversing Heart Disease*. New York: Ballantine Books, 1990.

Petrie, Sidney. *What Modern Hypnotism Can Do for You.* Greenwich, Connecticut: Fawcett Publications, 1968.

Progoff, Ira. *At a Journal Workshop.* New York: Putnam Publishing, 1991.

Rechtschaffen, Stephan. *Time Shifting.* New York: Bantam Books, 1996.

Riso, Don, and Russ Hudson. *Personality Types.* Revised edition. New York: Houghton-Mifflin, 1996.

Robbins, Anthony. *Awaken the Giant Within.* New York: Simon & Schuster, 1992.

————. *Unlimited Power.* New York: Simon & Schuster, 1992.

Roger, John. *Life 101.* Los Angeles: Prelude Press, 1994.

Siegel, Bernie S., MD. *Love, Medicine, and Miracles.* New York: Harper & Row, 1986.

————. *Peace, Love and Healing.* New York: Harper Perennial, 1989.

Simonton, Carl. *Getting Well Again.* New York: Bantam Books, 1980.

Sivananda Yoga Vedanta Center. *Learn Yoga in a Weekend.* New York: Alfred A. Knopf, 1980.

Wilde, Stuart. *Life Was Never Meant to Be a Struggle.* Carlsbad, California: Hay House, 1998.

Zinker, Joseph. *Creative Process in Gestalt Therapy.* New York: Random House, 1978.

Of Special Interest to Women:

Breathnach, Sarah Ban. *Simple Abundance.* New York:Warner Books, 1995.

Louden, Jennifer. *The Woman's Comfort Book.* New York: Harper San Francisco, 1992.

Of Special Interest to Men:

Bly, Robert. *Iron John.* Woburn, Massachusetts: Addison-Wesley, 1990.

Keen, Sam. *Fire in the Belly: On Becoming a Man.* New York: Bantam Doubleday Dell, 1992.

Tina Thomas is available for speaking engagements, keynote addresses, seminars, and other special presentations.
To find out how to schedule her for your organization's most important event(s), contact the author at:

Abita Springs Be & Be
75368 Moonshadow Lane
Abita Springs, LA 70420

To order additional copies of

A Gentle Path

Contact: BookPartners, Inc.
P.O. Box 922
Wilsonville, Oregon 97070
Phone: (503) 682-9821
Phone: 1-800-895-7323
Fax: (503) 682-8684
E-mail: bpbooks@teleport.com